# Just Visitin'
## Old Texas Jails

Joan Upton Hall

# Just Visitin'
## Old Texas Jails

**Joan Upton Hall**

State House
Press
McMurry University
Abilene, Texas

**Library of Congress CIP data**

Hall, Joan Upton.
    Just visitin': old Texas jails / Joan Upton Hall.
       p. cm.
    ISBN-13: 978-1-933337-14-2 (pbk.: alk. paper)
    ISBN-10: 1-933337-14-1 (pbk.: alk. paper)
1. Jails—Texas—History. 2. Jails—Texas—Design and construction.
I. Title.

HV8746.U62T694 2006
365'.34—dc22

                                             2006033175

State House Press
McMurry Station, Box 637
Abilene, TX 79697-0637
(325) 572-3974
(325) 572-3991 fax
www.mcwhiney.org/press

Distributed by Texas A&M University Press Consortium
1-800-826-8911
www.tamu.edu/upress

ISBN-10: 1-933337-14-1
ISBN-13: 978-1-933337-14-2
10 9 8 7 6 5 4 3 2 1

Book Design by Rosenbohm Graphic Design

# Table of Contents

# Illustrations

The map found on page 8 is by Robert F. Pace. All uncredited photographs were taken by Don Hall. Special thanks to all the historical organizations who provided the antique photographs used in the book.

# Locations of the *Just Visitin'* Jails

Mobeetie ●

□ Channing

● Silverton

Quanah

● Benjamin

● Henrietta

● Denison

△ New Boston

● Archer City

Fort Worth

□ McKinney

● Albany

□ Dallas

● Palo Pinto

□ Waxahachie

● Granbury

● Buffalo Gap

● Hillsboro

● Carthage

● Hico

● Fairfield

● San Elizario

● Monahans

Brownwood ●

● Hamilton

Goldthwaite □

● Gatesville

□ Centerville

● Brady

Llano

● Calvert

Kirbyville ●

△ Kent

● Fort Stockton

□ Ozona

Mason ●

□ Burnet

● Cameron

□ Georgetown

Fredericksburg □

● Austin

Bastrop

Blanco ●

San Marcos

● La Grange

● Bandera

● Lockhart

● Houston

● Boerne

Bellville ●

San Antonio ●

▲ Selma

● Gonzales

Richmond □

Moore △

● Floresville

● Wharton

● Pearsall & Frio Town

● Helena

● Edna

Beeville □

Key:
- ● Open to the public (42)
- □ Visited in the book, but not open to the public (14)
- ▲ Jails pretending (1)
- ♠ Former jail, but now private residence (1)
- △ Abandoned jails (3)

● Edinburg

*Robert F. Pace*

# Introduction

The classic board game Monopoly doesn't include a jail in its community for nothing. Jails hold a certain awe for most of us, and in the game or in reality, everyone would rather be "just visiting." Communities that have realized new uses for the old buildings are making that possible.

Whether you call it "hoosegow," "calaboose," or "correctional facility," as soon as a county seat was established, a lockup claimed top priority, sometimes even before the courthouse. Early Texas methods for incarcerating criminals sound extreme and inhuman by today's standards, but few law-abiding citizens lived much better themselves. They simply did the best they could. The first jails may have been little more than a chicken coop, but subsequent buildings remain today as architectural and historical attractions.

Why are so many of these structures beautiful as well as strong? Historians point out that builders took pride in the appearance because these symbols of authority had to excel in strength, meant to stand for generations. And stand many of them have. Considering the measures employed to make them escape proof, demolition of the buildings might wear out a wrecking ball or two. At least one jail laced its outer walls with small cannon balls mortared between the stone blocks, and others used steel pins. Other ingenious systems came into use such as metal cages within the walls that could be locked simultaneously without the jailer having to risk going inside. Bars were invented that could not be sawed through, and jailers devised surveillance devices to observe prisoner activity.

Apparently female offenders posed a quandary for law enforcers. Many jails had one separate cell dedicated to "lunatics and women," but the first death sentence for a woman did not come until 1933. Even then the woman "cheated the electric chair" by starving herself to death.

Quite a bit of writing turns up at the museums regarding the correct procedure for death by hanging, and one sheriff drew diagrams to show it. These explanations did not result from sadistic preoccupation, but from a genuine concern to make the execution as quick and painless as possible. The expression, "dancing at the end of a rope," meant the person died of slow strangulation.

Why aren't these jails still employed for their original intention? Since the jails cannot be upgraded to today's incarceration standards, or because the smaller sized buildings pose a threat to the jailers' safety, many are converted into other revenue streams. Unrecognized as the valuable resources they are, quite a few still stand neglected to the point of ruin, or are relegated to mere storage facilities. Some have even been destroyed.

But thanks to innovative minds with an appreciation for history, the jails featured in this book have realized their potential as town attractions. Aren't we all curious about the stories those mighty walls could tell? And hearing the stories, don't we want to see what it's like inside those walls? How fitting that the buildings which once kept folks safe from outlaws now serve us as museums, libraries, restaurants, hotels or B&Bs, and even homes. Former jails in the main section of this book open their doors to the public, one dating as far back as 1850. Those in the end section may not offer public accessibility (at least not at this point), but they do demonstrate other adaptive uses.

"Just visiting," as the old Monopoly game called it, takes on a more enjoyable meaning as you come along on an imaginary or physical excursion to the places that interest you most. Included here is but a sampling of facilities located across Texas. At last, you can go to jail and like it!

# Common Practices and Situations

Before a jail was built, lawmen commonly hired citizens to guard prisoners and possibly to rent them for labor. Sometimes they were "ironed" (see Glossary) and chained to a wall or floor ring. Lacking a cage of any kind, they might be tied to a tree or pole, prey to animal predators on the frontier. Ysleta, Texas, is said to have even used old fashioned stocks or steel bars manufactured with oil in a particular way to make them saw proof.

Early records, where they exist, show a great many escapes and recaptures. This might have something to do with the fact that a sheriff could earn about $10 for recapturing a prisoner, whereas arresting one was just expected as part of the job. Most early sheriffs had the additional job of tax assessor collector, which was a welcome supplement to the small income they received for risking their lives.

Following the Civil War, the Reconstruction period of 1865-1870s (longer in some places than others) rendered countless Southerners homeless and jobless. Texas, less ravaged than other states by the war, was afterward ravaged by an influx of desperadoes to a largely ungoverned area. Some outlaws left "Indian sign" at the sites of their murders to divert revenge onto Native Americans (see Boerne chapter). Other people looking for new opportunities also emigrated, and "Gone to Texas" became a common saying. Former slaves with no experience in making their own way were exploited by both northern carpetbaggers and local scalawags.

Reconstruction governors appointed sheriffs rather than allowing citizens to elect them. This caused much resentment and resulted in so much violence that few sheriffs completed a term (commonly recorded as "resigned" or "failed to qualify"). Citizens often resorted to vigilante justice, such as the Ku Klux Klan, which was anything but "just." The KKK persecuted various groups, just about anyone who looked different from the faces they saw in the mirror (see the San Marcos chapter and the Bellville chapter for particular instances).

Some jails look similar to others, mainly because there was a limited number of builders, and the patented hardware sometimes dictated how the outer construction would look (see Brady chapter). As jail building became a specialty, the issue of keeping a permanent jailer on the premises was answered by providing an apartment, usually on the ground floor, for the family of a sheriff or jailer. This also provided a permanent cook, the jailer's wife, who received a small allowance for each prisoner she fed (see Bastrop chapter).

As Texas Rangers and county sheriffs gradually tamed the frontier, proper hanging became a concern. If the neck was broken at the first vertebrae, death would be quicker. It did not always work that way as several chapters show.

Public outdoor hangings typically drew large crowds. It was a time for family picnics, and photographers took pictures to sell as keepsakes (see Bellville chapter). To deter the carnival mood regarding executions, indoor gallows became common. These gallows were placed in the highest position available, such as a tower. In other cases, the highest point was the second floor having an open space with a trapdoor to drop the prisoner to the lower floor. If this were not a sufficient drop to break his neck, the executioner had to provide a hanging hole to make up the rest of the distance (see Fairfield chapter). The jail at Mobeetie solved the problem with a portable hanging device they could set up wherever space allowed.

Execution methods have changed through the years, varying from state to state. Firing squads of very early times or in the military gave way to hanging; hanging continued until 1923; the electric chair went from then until about 1977, and then yielded to lethal injection or gassing.

The Glossary explains terms and gives pictorial explanation.

**Note:** Because most of the vintage buildings still surviving have done so partly with the help of awards, such as the National Register of Historic Places and Texas Historical Landmark, every award has not been reiterated. The awards, however, are no less appreciated.

*Shackelford County Jail in the early 20th Century,*
*Courtesy of Old Jail Art Center, Albany, Texas.*

# Albany
# Shackelford County Jail
## (1878-1929)
## Old Jail Art Center

The Shackelford County Jail at Albany takes the cake for the most extreme personality change—successful, that is. It's now nationally accredited by the American Association of Art Museums and receives tens of thousands of visitors each year. When you go through the courtyard, tastefully appointed with sculpture, and enter this highly sophisticated building, you know the resident prisoners of long ago wouldn't recognize it. Along with furnishings of historical importance to the region, you'll see art from Pre-Columbian times to modern. Some of the artists' names are household words.

A video presentation gives an overview of the diverse history of the region to get the visitor oriented. The California Gold Rush and later hard times following the Civil War brought a surge of people through Texas's frontier. One of the string of forts that grew up to defend pioneers was Fort Griffin, established in 1867 before there was a town of Albany.

Settlers, however, called Fort Griffin the "Babylon of the Prairies," and if you look at the tiny Fort Griffin Jail, now sitting in Albany's City Park, you have to agree authorities must not have intended to lock up many law breakers. Civilians ranged from "lewd women" (one has to wonder if there weren't also a few lewd men) to buffalo hunters, gamblers, and gunfighters unaccustomed to civilization. Honest, hard-working families could count on little protection from the law. In 1874, they established the town of Albany "at the end of the tracks." Then the railroad relocated through Abilene, leaving citizens high and dry. Their only recourse "to take care of outlaws" was vigilante justice, and in some cases this "care" was in the outlaw's favor due to friend and family loyalties.

The town's founding fathers asked for a two-story jail to be built the same year as the courthouse. The jail was to contain "two commodius rooms on the lower story" and cells for prisoners on the upper story with a patented locking system that claimed to prevent escapes (this locking system no longer there). Their goal was not to exceed $3,500 in construction costs, but they agreed to $8,000. They ended up paying even more than that as unforeseen expenses arose.

It took a year to build the jail, and the costs for the care and feeding of guards and prisoners "became onerous." The architect, who was building several other jails at the same time, had financial difficulties of his own, and was unable to pay the builders regularly. Therefore, various local stone masons laid claim to their work by carving their initials into the huge limestone blocks as a record for payment later. To this day you can tell when the operation became solvent by the absence of stone masons' initials in the upper layers.

Best seen from the courtyard is the "hanging door," which is no longer functional. Its operation was simple. A prisoner, with noose fitted around his neck, would be pushed out the door to fall one and a half stories before coming to an abrupt halt.

The jailer and his family lived in two downstairs rooms. Prisoners were incarcerated upstairs in four cells that had a walkway around them. The barred windows had no glass. Wooden shutters provided temperature control, and the only heat came from the two downstairs fireplaces by way of the chimneys joining in the center. Not until around the turn of the century was glass fitted into the windows and wood-burning stoves installed.

One of the town's darkest stories involved John Larn, a notorious former Shackelford County Sheriff, and his friend John Selman. Often in trouble, the two were accused of murder and cattle rustling by the Tin Hat Band, a group of local vigilantes. Selman escaped, but Larn was arrested and taken to the county jail by W.R. Cruger, the Sheriff who succeeded him. Since the jail was not very secure at that time, Sheriff Cruger told the blacksmith to shackle Larn to a ring in the stone fireplace. Late in the night a group of masked men broke into the jail. They shot and killed Larn in his chains. The identity of these men remains a matter of speculation as no one was charged with the "informal execution."

Selman meanwhile had fled into New Mexico where he took up with Billy the Kid. In 1880, Texas Rangers captured him in El Paso and brought him back to the Shackelford County Jail for trial. His guards escorted him to Fort Griffin on the pretense of meeting with his lawyer. Instead, for some unknown reason, they gave him a horse, a gun, and his freedom. In 1896 in El Paso, Selman gunned down the infamous John Wesley Hardin, and another man returned the favor for him. Some sources report that Hardin had previously served time in the Shackelford County Jail.

Another hapless prisoner, who left his autograph "J. Haydin" carved into the plaster, deserves more sympathy. Previously a cook at Albany's Sackett Hotel, he had been charged with assault and intent to murder. He was found not guilty after an 18-month stay. Only that one square of graffiti remains.

The north fence of the Marshall Young Courtyard is made from cell bars removed from the building. Most dramatic of the few key features that remind us today that this building was a jail is a massive barred door that leads upstairs. Otherwise, the building is totally redesigned to accommodate the extensive art collection and display of historical artifacts.

As a jail, it served until replaced in 1929. Other than having a few homeless families to take refuge there, it stood empty until 1948 when it was threatened with demolition. To save it, writer Robert Nail, Jr., purchased it to use as his studio. He paid $375 for the building, later having to pay an additional $25 for the land. There he stored his historical documents, photographs, and other collections.

This was the place where Nail, already a published author, created a play for the high school senior fund raiser. "Dr. Shackelford's Paradise" depicted the county's history in the form of a musical production. In 1938 the townspeople expanded it to the "Fort Griffin Fandangle," and it has been the main tourist draw for Albany's annual celebration ever since.

Besides leaving this legacy to the town when he died in 1968, Nail left the Old Jail building to his nephew, Reilly Nail. An art collector, Reilly persuaded other collectors to pledge a portion of their collections to turn the building into a small art museum. It opened to an enthusiastic audience in 1980. Expansions added in 1984 and 1996 have increased the space to over 14,000 square feet.

The historical building has earned state and national awards. The Nail family deeded the building to the Old Jail Foundation, a not-for-profit corporation that also maintains the Green Art Research Library and provides on-going educational programs for both youth and adults. Not bad for a small town hoosegow. And art is much better to hang than people.

For information about visiting times or tours, contact: Old Jail Art Center, 201 S. Second Street, Albany, TX 76430. (325) 762-2269, ojac@camalott.com

*Old Fort Griffin Jail, now in the city park.*

*Shackelford County Jail current appearance.*

*Archer County Jail circa 1910. Courtesy of the Archer County Historical Commission.*

## Archer City
# Archer County Jail
## (1910-1974)
### Archer County Historical Jail Museum

Archer City has its ironies. The town that inspired Larry McMurtry's award-winning book and movie, *The Last Picture Show* (and thus saved the theater), was the same town that built the last hanging gallows in Texas in its new jail only thirteen years before that method of execution was changed. And like the Royal Theater of "last picture show" fame, which is in fact thriving, the old county jail is a tourist resource just beginning to be fully appreciated.

A previous jail had been merely sixteen-feet square and six-feet high. Made of boards nailed flat on top of each other to discourage prying them loose, it had been windowless and possessed one locked door.

The 1910 three-story jail, built of native sandstone, was an impressive replacement, and prisoners should have appreciated the improvement of tall windows. Some certainly did, but not just for ventilation. Four or five escapes took place by sawing through the bars of those windows. Head of the Archer County Historical Commission, Jack Loftin, however, goes on to explain in his book *Trails Through Archer* that would-be escape artists in the inside cells, met with frustration when they tried the same thing. These cells had rolling stock (See Glossary).

Loftin's wife, Marie, was the daughter of Sheriff Curg (C.P.) Pryor, and she lived in the first floor sheriff's quarters from 1939 through 1942, along with her seven sisters and brothers. She remembers her mother keeping records for the side-line job of tax assessor-collector. She also remembers prisoners dropping money for her and the other kids playing in the yard to go and buy food for them.

Everybody knew Sheriff Pryor wouldn't put up with disorderly conduct and didn't hesitate to use his billie club and brass knuckles if a situation warranted it. But prisoners also knew he was fair if they cooperated. Marie says he considered most of them as "good people who had made bad choices," and he would allow the more trustworthy prisoners to attend public functions. What's more, townspeople who were arrested for drunken behavior were allowed to eat with the family and sleep in beds downstairs to keep them separated from "real" criminals. Pryor even gave guns to certain prisoners to shoot pigeons through the barred, upstairs windows.

Marie tells of one time when the truck came from Huntsville to take a convicted criminal to the state penitentiary. Her daddy told the officers, "He's over at the courthouse lawn eating watermelon." When the officers put leg irons on him and hauled him away, Marie and the other kids cried.

Whether the jail was ever crowded is unclear, but according to records, these were the years when the jail had the most prisoners. The average number during the jail's sixty-four years of service was about 130 prisoners a year, and not all of them were as nice as a child's viewpoint would have them. The sad irony of how an earlier lawman was killed in the line of duty is recorded on a monument standing on the courthouse grounds. In a 1925 gun battle, Sheriff Harrison Ikard was fatally shot by thieves over cases of stolen cigarettes.

When a newer jail was built in 1974, the one built in 1910 closed. Almost immediately the American Legion bought it for a dollar, and the Historical Commission (then called the Archer County Survey Commission) turned it into a museum the very next year. Volunteers kept it open to the public until a full-time curator was hired in 1977. Through the years almost 3,000 relics have been contributed by gift or loan for the exhibits. These range from kitchen utensils to farm machinery.

Do any ghosts of the former residents haunt the property? Some of the museum volunteers feel a presence occasionally, but no one has ever suggested who it might be or investigated the possibility. One volunteer felt more than the usual "presence." She was sweeping the concrete stairs from the second floor down. The space is close to a first floor cell, and she had to back up to it. From behind her, a pair of strong hands gripped her hips. She whirled around, and the hands let go. Although she saw no one through the bars, she sensed that the cell was occupied. This dauntless volunteer says she continues to work in the museum, but she hasn't turned her back to the cells since then.

Oil business and railroads had brought prosperity to Archer City during the first half of the twentieth century. Unfortunately, when the town began to decline in the 1960s, fewer visitors came, and the museum declined, too. Larry McMurtry captured the general demise symbolically in the closing of the Royal Theater as the end of an era. *The Last Picture Show* reawakened the town on a small scale and the rest of the nation on a large scale. The same little town that was able to rally its citizens to rebuild the Royal Theater into the year-round success it has become is beginning to realize the architectural treasure of the jail building that preserves and explains the area's past. With business again prospering, the Archer County Historical Museum welcomes visitors.

The Archer County Historical Museum is located at 400 W. Pecan St., just up the street from the courthouse square. For information about visiting times or tours, contact: Archer Community Foundation, Royal Theater/Walsh Park Visitor Center. (940) 574-2489 or (877) 729-7692 or visit their website at: www.royaltheater.org

*Archer County Jail current appearance. Stacey Hasbrook photographer.*

*Travis County Courthouse housing upstairs former jail.*

# Austin
# Travis County Jail
## (1931-1990)
## Training Facility & Haunted Jail Tour

I had almost given up finding an old jail in Austin after questioning two historical organizations and a few law officers. Little did I know a 1931 jail is hidden in the middle of the city.

Serving on a bookstore panel, I met Greg Lawson, mystery writer and Travis County sheriff's deputy, who told me about the old jail, in the top two floors of the existing courthouse. As Firearms Range Master, he knows the labyrinth-like facility well because that's where he trains recruits to avoid getting shot while pursuing lawbreakers. He had us meet him several days later to tour the old place and let my husband Don take photos.

I feared this jail wouldn't fit the criteria as something the public could visit, but I learned otherwise. Any abandoned jail is eerie, but this place had remnants of Halloween decorations from the Haunted Jail Tour they do annually. Pushing through fake cobwebs, Lawson told us we should see it when some of the jailers become ghouls for the event. I will definitely be there for the next one.

Something I hadn't expected was a series of large, artistic wall murals, featuring nature scenes and animals. Each was signed simply "lorenzo," all lowercase. Although he must have been a trustee, whatever crime he did kept him locked up long enough to get a sizeable amount of painting done.

The jail is more modern than most in this book. It has a padded cell, with a hole in the floor in lieu of a plumbing fixture an inmate could hurt himself on. There's a medical facility, attorney interview room, and a shelf for a TV in a ten-bunk room for trustees. We observed where all the bars had been sawed out of an outside window to meet fire code requirements, and a food chute in a steel door welded shut because of its potential for slamming a hand. The county did what they could to keep the old building up to standards.

The local government began hiring women officers and found them to be quite competent. Lt. Debra Galloway told of one burly athlete incarcerated on rape charges "in the days we called it what it was." He enjoyed performing lewd acts in front of the female officers. She didn't give him the satisfaction of acting shocked or intimidated.

Another guy had murdered his toddler niece, claiming that voices told him she was the devil. Grasping the little girl's legs, he had swung her like a baseball bat against the walls. He was placed in an isolation cell where an officer checked him every fifteen minutes. On one of these checks, the officer saw the inmate trying to gouge out his own eye and radioed for assistance as required. When they got to him, it was too late. He had squashed the eyeball like a grape. Galloway saw him being taken to the hospital, restrained to keep him from removing his other eye as well.

Capt. Peggy Hill recalls that working the shift on quiet nights wasn't bad. The windows on these top floors allowed a detached view of the city. One night, Willie Nelson and members of his band paid a visit, serenading officers and prisoners alike.

Other times were unpleasant, and certain frequent "guests" took advantage of fair treatment. One of these had been a pro boxer, sent from the city jail fully restrained in leg irons and handcuffs because he was so dangerous. During fingerprinting, he convinced the officer to uncuff him, and then punched the officer in the face, knocking him out cold.

Another repeat inmate, a female we'll call "Miss C." (for "Congeniality" if you like) could never get along with other inmates and had to have a cell to herself. Nevertheless, officers treated her fairly, and like other inmates, she had been given a gallon jug of tea to sip during the day. She became so unruly, the officer on duty tried unsuccessfully to move her to the padded cell. When Capt. Hill reported for duty, the two officers worked together to do the job and Hill entered the cell. Miss C. dumped her gallon jug on Hill, contents she'd been collecting all day, and it wasn't tea. The two officers got Miss C. in the padded cell before Hill could clean herself up.

Hill says her husband, an Austin firefighter, told her they all dreaded responding to a call in the jail. Besides doing their job, they had to watch out for inmates grabbing them from the cells in the narrow walkways or "cat-walks" as the jail officers called them. Once, one firefighter left his ax in the cat-walk and didn't realize it until later. Fortunately, no prisoner was able to reach it.

I heard several references to the big riot and fire of 1981. Maj. David Balagia says he was off-duty when it started. He and a co-worker came in from playing tennis and saw the event unfolding on TV. They drove to the jail to help, but by the time they arrived it was over. Instead of doing something heroic, they were handed mops to help clean up the water! He doesn't remember what the prisoners were angry about that time, but says fire-starting seemed almost routine then. The incarcerated had discovered that the plentiful pigeon droppings were flammable. Balagia says when you're outside, look up to the courthouse's fifth and sixth floors. You'll see this is a favorite roost for pigeons, and they still get into the jail.

Eventually in the seventies, a prisoner named Leon Musgrove started a lawsuit that found the facility unconstitutional on several points. By 1986 a new jail had been built, but due to inmate overcrowding, the county didn't close the one built in 1931 until 1990. All the locks were removed or dismantled at that time.

Balagia says he was glad to see it go for the sake of the jailers. When he talked about too many blind spots, it reminded me of Lawson's saying that if an officer can make it through this place in training drills without getting paint-balled, he has a good chance of evading a bullet during a pursuit. With all the unpleasantness law officers deal with, it's refreshing to see how the good ones manage to keep their sense of humor and continue to care about decent people.

Captain Hill is in charge of the Jailer's Association fundraiser, the "Haunted Tour." Proceeds go mostly to the Sheriff's Memorial Benevolent Society (SMBS) with a portion going to the Travis County Combined Charities Festival. The project has been so successful the group not only wants to continue the event, but expand it. Originally for county employees, they now invite the public and offer it more days, depending on commitment from volunteers.

Officer Belinda Redpath says the idea started with the premise that, when the jail closed, what if there were officers and inmates left who couldn't get out? One year she wore a T-shirt she'd bought on a visit to Alcatraz, but she'd changed the logo to "Alcatravis." So many people wanted to buy shirts like it, the group is now selling them.

Tracy Hill, a second-generation officer, told how the officers have as much fun with the tour as the visitors do. One year her costume was that of a ghoulish "psych" inmate while her mother, Peggy, played a "deceased officer." They decided to play a trick on the officers working security at the barbeque area outside the entrance by staging an escape. Tracy ran outside dragging a leg-iron with Peggy chasing and yelling, "Escapee!" Five officers in civilian clothes and another in uniform met them. When one started to draw down on her, Tracy threw up her hands and shouted, "Just kidding! Don't shoot!" None of them needed white makeup after that.

Captain Hill cautions that the tour is too loud and scary for very young children, and since this is an old jail with no elevators, it is not handicap accessible.

The courthouse is located at Eleventh and Guadalupe Streets. For information about tours, contact: SMBS, Haunted Tour Fund Raiser, P.O. Box 252, Del Valle, TX 78617. Details will be updated on the website. Visit www.tcsheriff.org, click "links and resources," and scroll down to Sheriff's Benevolent Fund.

*One of several paintings by 'lorenzo' found in the Travis County Jail.*

*Bandera County Jail circa 1890 with one-armed Sheriff V.P. Sandidge, "tougher than any two-armed man" (others unidentified). Courtesy Bandera County Historical Commission.*

# Bandera
# Bandera County Jail
## (1881-1938)
### Old Bandera Jail Museum

Bandera's town motto is "The Cowboy Capital of the World," which even for Texas sounds like an audacious claim. But the more I found out, the more I agreed there's a larger than life, Wild West aspect about the whole county.

More than one officer has been killed or maimed in the line of duty. Deputy Sheriff Jack Phillips, who had led a company of Indian fighters in the early 1860s, was the last Banderan killed by Indians when they caught him alone in 1877 or 1878. In 1932, Sheriff Elvious Hicks was ambushed and killed, allegedly by bootleggers, during his third term in office. A more recent officer, Johnny Saul, was "luckier." As he walked into a bar one night, somebody blew his arm off with a shotgun. Bandera County Historical

Commission president, Dan Wise, told of another one-armed man, Sheriff V.P. Sandidge, "who was said to be tougher than any man with two arms."

Fortunately, the good guys won most of the time. About 1912, when Sheriff Sam Smith personally went to pick up a prisoner, he created quite a stir in California, a state with its own share of Wild West types. The prisoner had a bad habit of committing check frauds and escapes. Articles in an Oakland newspaper called Smith the "Cattle Rustlers' Terror," and said he'd "been in more daring escapades and captures than any public officer today." The article pictured him and described: ". . . strapped to a belt of monster proportions, was a holster containing a Colt .45 caliber that resembled a small rifle" with which "he could shoot the ace out of a card at 100 yards."

One look at the 1881 jail with its battlements across the top and its fine arched windows told us this was no ordinary building, despite its rather small size. Compared with the first calaboose, however, it must have looked gigantic. County records report that the first jail had been a square wood-plank structure no larger than an average bedroom. The single door was a hole in the roof that could be accessed by a ladder to be pulled up when prisoners weren't coming or going, and no one ever got out without the jailer's permission. As with other single room hoosegows, the worst bad guys had to be chained to a ring bolted to the floor to protect the others.

When the county replaced that jail, they hired the renowned architect Alfred Giles to design a smaller copy of the Bexar County Jail in San Antonio. This put the 1877 courthouse next door to shame, which Peggy Tobin in the *Bandera County Historian* (Summer 1979) called "the homely little building on the bluff." Unlike most jails, there was very little provision for the Sheriff's family to live in the jail, although Sheriff Sam Smith's sons did make a bedroom in part of the building during his tenure (1905-1917).

Instead the sheriffs' families lived in the old courthouse. Smith's youngest daughter Mellie was born there. As an adult, Mellie Smith Weed told reporters about her happy childhood, often helping her father feed the prisoners and sneaking into the jail with her sisters to talk to them when their father wasn't looking. As times changed, the county required a bigger, more modern jail, and the old structure was closed down in 1938.

The iron cages are now gone. They were donated to the government in 1942 for World War II materials, but one can see where they had been and imagine the typical scene. Most of the time, prisoners would have been allowed to move about in the runaround, now just a large meeting room. If the sheriff needed to enter, he ordered all inmates to go into the cells. Then he would lock them in by means of a lever outside the iron door.

Pictures carved into the floor's large stone blocks provided an unusual form of graffiti. One simple carving was "Crowbar Hotel." I asked our guide Susan Queen of the county office that now occupies the building if they knew who did the carvings. She explained that a lot of the jail records were lost, so they couldn't match any names to the pictures, but enough of the drawings were signed "Texas Davey Wayne" to make us wonder what he'd done to have that much time in the joint.

Another prisoner, motivated more by the love of freedom than art, had spent his carving efforts scraping out mortar with a spoon so he could push out one of the massive blocks and crawl out. His escape plan didn't succeed, but that of another inmate did—repeatedly. The man would climb the cell bars each night and go out through the tin ceiling. After spending the night at home, he'd come back in the morning before he was missed.

My standard question, "Are there any rumors of ghosts here?" met with a resounding "Oh, yeah!" from the staff. Janitors, who started out working at night, switched to daytime after one or two incidents. So many strange things happened, the skeptical manager of the company set up a motion-activated video camera to catch whoever was playing tricks on the staff. It came on all right, but nobody was there. News reporter Stephanie Logue spent a night in the jail as well as doing further investigation and wrote a full account for her newspaper and another version of it for *Ghostly Tales from America's Jails*. She thinks she has figured out who the ghost is, and although he never does anything to harm anybody, it is unnerving to be locked in the bathroom. I may yet have to spend a night in that jail and check out her story.

We talked to more recent sheriffs, who came in after the 1881 jail had been closed, and found they too seemed larger than life. Former Sheriff Guy Pickett, eighty-one at the time of our interview, said he had started out as the postmaster, because only when he started getting a retirement check for that, could he afford to seek the office of sheriff. Ironically, his retirement check was at least twice the check he got per month as sheriff.

James MacMillan, the sheriff who replaced Sheriff Pickett when he retired, had been Pickett's deputy, and together the two had plenty of humorous stories to tell. I sensed, however, that neither man was to be taken lightly. A convicted strong-armed robber from San Antonio, who had later "worked his way" into the Bandera County Jail, was so cooperative they made him a trustee. Sheriff MacMillan said, "I think he was scared of what to expect from us country boys."

Currently housing offices of the Bandera County River Authority and Ground Water District, the old jail is about to change to a museum operated by Bandera County Historical Commission. Look for the jail, set back from the road at 202 Twelfth Street. For information about visiting times or tours, contact: The Bandera County Historical Commission President at: (830) 796-9979.

*Bandera County Jail current appearance.*

# Bastrop
# Bastrop County Jail
## (1892-1974)
### City and county offices

One of the oldest settlements in Texas, part of Stephen F. Austin's 1827 colony, was Bastrop. It officially became a town in 1832 under a different name when Texas was still part of Mexico. But for a town that old and wild, it was slow in building the sturdy jail we see today, though a couple of hoosegows had preceded it. The Carpetbagger period of 1865-1872 didn't help the town's stability. Current Sheriff Richard Hernandez reports that through the years, shootings were common, and a vigilante group in the nearby town of McDade took their self-appointed job so seriously it wasn't uncommon "to ride into town and see neighbors or outlaws hanging from trees."

Militias had to be called in twice to quell "civilian violence." At last in 1892, the county built a jail. The second and third floor held cells mostly for men (sometimes sixty at a time), two separate cells for women and the criminally insane, and "the hole" for solitary confinement. Hernandez commented, "In those days, there was no such thing as overcrowding as long as a mattress could be found."

Records show the predominant crime was horse-thieving until enforcement of the "Sunday Law" resulted in a higher number of arrests for "playing cards, betting, disturbing Sunday worship, carrying a pistol," plus one indictment for "seduction." During Prohibition, the crime with the highest incidence became bootlegging.

Of course, there were more serious crimes. Murderers were usually sentenced to the penitentiary for twenty-five years to life, but the new jail didn't have long to wait before the initiation of its gallows. Mounted in the ceiling of a two-story high steeple, was a large hook for the hangman's rope. A wooden scaffold with a trapdoor would be positioned directly in line with the noose allowing for an eight-foot drop. Not all the records survived the move to the new jail, and although there are many tales of hangings, only two are documented, both described in great detail by the *Bastrop Advertiser*, Texas's oldest continuing weekly newspaper.

In 1892, Tobe Cook had been found guilty of a rape-murder, though even the newspaper editor commented that the evidence was purely circumstantial. When the Judge asked the defendant if he had anything to say before sentencing, Cook said, "I am as innocent . . . of the murder of Miss Bell as the hair on your head . . ." Nevertheless, the judge sentenced him to be "hanged by the neck until dead, dead, dead!" The time it took, from the trapdoor's fall to the doctor's pronouncement that his heart had finally stopped beating, was thirty-three minutes.

The very next year, a man named Alec Brown was also found guilty of murdering a woman in a manner he confessed to be premeditated and cold-blooded. He was pronounced dead after "only" fifteen minutes.

Accounts from employees and family members of various sheriffs present a more pleasant side of the old jail. Before the first floor was partitioned into offices as it is now, the sheriff's family home had four bedrooms and a bathroom. The sheriff's wife, sometimes with the help of another cook and perhaps a trustee, prepared the meals. The family, deputies, and frequent visitors ate the same fare as the prisoners except for some additional meat and an occasional dessert. The family usually raised a large garden, which helped augment the 90 cents a day allowance per prisoner (later raised to $1.25).

Lettie B. Hall, a cook at the jail during the Depression, said, "Prisoners were fed good. Some of them *wanted* to get in jail." No evening meal was served, however, unless a prisoner's family or friends brought it to him. In those hard times, so-called "hoboes," or homeless people, were fed and allowed to come in out of the cold where they could sleep near the heater. Most would return the favor by working.

Sheriff Edward Cartwright made the jail his family's home for his entire term, 1933-1953. Ethel, his daughter, said she lived in the jail from the age of twelve to twenty. She remembered the pride of being introduced at school as "the high sheriff's daughter." Another high point in her memory was how rich the family felt when the county started paying her father a salary of $90 a month. Up to that time, sheriffs used their own automobiles and bought their own weapons and ammunition. The sheriff's real wages came from commissions earned for actual duties they performed (marriages, tax collecting, etc.), and mileage logged for going to pick up prisoners at a nickel a mile and returning with the prisoner at a quarter a mile.

As Ethel grew up, she would go with her father on long trips to pick up prisoners who were extradited for crimes they had committed in Bastrop County. Those incidents didn't frighten her, but others did. Once the FBI called and told Sheriff Cartwright to set up a road block for Bonnie and Clyde, who were supposedly coming that way. As the sheriff said, "It's my .45 against their backseat full of automatic weapons." Luckily, Bonnie and Clyde didn't show up.

Another time, a mob threatened to break in and lynch a prisoner. Sheriff Cartwright held his ground. "He's my prisoner, and he deserves a trial. I can't shoot 'em all, but I'll get some before they get me." The mob backed down, and though the prisoner was later electrocuted at Huntsville, he got his fair trial first.

As a young lady, Ethel began dating Warren Higgins, her future husband. Since the jail had to be locked at all times, to let Ethel back in, Warren would be given a key so big and heavy it would barely fit in his coat pocket.

Another sheriff's "kid," Ricky Hoskins, told about his dad, Sheriff Ira Raymond Hoskins, who served three separate terms and contributed a lasting journal by writing "Jail House News" for the newspaper. In it he interspersed history with such observations as, "Mondays usually are [quiet]. It runs kindly like snakes and lizards after a bad winter [the weekend]."

Ricky related, "I was sort of the recreation officer." Playing in the yard, he would throw a baseball for prisoners to catch and throw back. When no prisoners were in jail, he and his friends were allowed to play cops and robbers in the jail, even taking turns locking each other up. "The only jail break was mine," Ricky said. He was quite young when his mother once had to stay in the hospital at Austin. Ricky didn't know where that was, but he wanted to see her so he took off on his Shetland pony. Fortunately, his older brother, working at a filling station, saw him galloping past and brought him back to jail. Later his dad took him to visit his mother.

Ricky said his dad received many a threatening phone call, but would always respond, "You know where I live." Sheriff Hoskins never had to fire a shot. His billy club or the butt of his gun was all he needed. Sheriff Hoskins had started off in law enforcement at age eighteen, guarding penitentiary work details in Sugarland, and he died in office as sheriff in 1987. His three terms totaled thirty-six years.

I asked various interviewees my usual question about rumors of hauntings. Most said no, but some of the office workers admitted to eerie noises and feelings. The only definite "sighting" had been recorded by Sheriff James Nutt (tenure 1960-1980).

One evening Sheriff Nutt sent two trustees to the second floor on an errand, unaware that a prisoner had escaped his cell and gone into the attic with the plan to drop outside the walls to freedom. Instead he dropped in front of the two trustees who were standing below the ceiling steeple with its hanging hook. In the dim light, the very thin white man, in white tee-shirt and light trousers, looked to the trustees like the ghost of a hanged man. One of them fainted.

By 1974 the old jail had housed its last prisoner. Today the jail is occupied by various city and county offices, an office for the area Texas Ranger, and a jury deliberation room.

The old jail is located on the corner of Water and Pine Streets beside the courthouse. Groups such as school classes can arrange for tours of the upstairs jail. For information, contact the Bastrop Museum Director at (512) 303-3389 or visit their website at: www.bastroptexas.net/around_bastrop

*Bastrop County Jail current appearance.*

*Austin County Jail circa 1895. A commercial photographer sold pictures at the double hanging. Courtesy of Bellville Historical Society.*

## Bellville
# Austin County Jail
## (1896-1982)
### Austin County Jail Museum
### & Visitor's Center

The Romanesque revival style Austin County Jail is an ominous sight, but upon entering, I experienced a sense of warm welcome in what had been the jailer's living quarters. Furnishings left by former occupants set the tone for grace, such as a pump organ nestled under the stairs in the wide entry hall.

When John Sauer, Chairman of the jail museum, unlocked the huge boiler-plate door that led up to the cells, all feeling of hospitality fled, and the hair on the back of my neck stood up. A noosed rope hangs from the turret in the stairwell, used only once in 1901. Helen Alexander, a museum worker, had set up interviews with people who actually lived or worked in the jail, so I was treated to an emotional roller coaster ride of stories ranging from tales of kindness and comedy to the darkly sinister.

Four earlier jails had been built on the same spot, and in those days it was common for citizens to hire prisoners for work details. From descriptions of the older jail in Isabel Frizzell's *Bellville, The Founders and Their Legacy* a work detail was much preferred over time spent in the old lockup.

When the fortress-like jail was built in 1896, the sheriff's quarters sat unoccupied until Sheriff Albert Remmert (tenure 1921-1935) moved his family in. By 1925, two bedrooms were created upstairs to accommodate the family more comfortably. The same remodeling project provided steam heat for the prisoners.

Sheriff Remmert's daughter Isabel (now Isabel Frizzell) grew up in the jail from the age of two to twelve. She remembers her friends loved to come over, so fascinated by the jail they would barely play. Inmates sometimes talked to the children from the upstairs windows, never rudely.

As Isabel grew older, she realized the danger of her father's job. In 1922, with anti-German sentiments running high, a family feud between two prominent families at Sealy, also in Austin County, resulted in deaths from each faction. At one funeral, robed members of the Bellville Ku Klux Klan placed a wreath on the grave, and tension increased. Texas Rangers joined with Sheriff Remmert, Sheriff Parker of Brenham, and their officers to control the situation.

A group of Sealy citizens informed Remmert of a planned KKK parade. He posted a proclamation in Sealy, forbidding the demonstration of men in masks or in disguise. Other lawmen had been shot attempting to stop a KKK parade, but fortunately, armed supporters of the sheriff stationed themselves on rooftops on the parade route, and it did not materialize.

Chief Deputy "Cotton" Noviskie served as jailer from 1960 to the jail's closing in 1982. His widow, whom people still call "Miss Pearl" (now Pearl Meyer), related what it was like to be a jailer's wife. Officer John Henry Girndt, who had served with Noviskie, said that before the walls were lined with sheet metal it was hard to keep prisoners inside the run-down jail. While they were in the runaround surrounding the cells, they scraped out the old mortar between stones with such implements as plastic spoons and metal slats broken from their cots. One prisoner dug his way out with a chicken bone. Cotton, so called for his thick white hair, regularly went out to check for sheets hanging from the windows. Once when Cotton opened the metal door, a prisoner hit him over the head with a broken-off table leg. He and the officer with him managed to get the prisoner locked back in his cell before Cotton went to the hospital.

Among the long-term prisoners, some became trustees. One in particular had supposedly killed three people, but he never exhibited a bad temper while the jailers knew him. Jesse (real name withheld) was deaf, but he communicated with Cotton and his deputy by a sign language all their own. He did painting and repair, and thanks to his gardening, the jail once was named the "Yard of the Month." Best of all, Jesse once warned Cotton to do a shake-down, and Cotton confiscated two makeshift knives made from metal cot slats. These "shanks" are on display at the museum.

When Jesse wanted to marry his fiancé, Judge Frizzell came to jail to perform the ceremony. Miss Pearl provided a wedding cake, flowers, and punch. Cotton took Jesse, his bride, and his whole family to the café for dinner. After the celebration was over, Jesse went back to his cell. His bride got into the decorated car and drove home.

At Jesse's retrial, Cotton had to do the talking, testifying that Jesse was a model prisoner, and without proof of his guilt, he was acquitted.

Officer Girndt praised Miss Pearl's cooking, recalling a framed note on exhibit in the museum. The note, signed by seven prisoners, reads: "Mrs. Noviskie, We are writing this note to say that we appreciate the food we have been receiving and tonight dinner was exceptionally good. Thank you."

But cooking wasn't all Miss Pearl did. She helped her law-enforcement husband on occasion. Once she drove their private car past a marijuana farm while officers in the backseat kept of sight until they could jump out and raid the location.

Officer Girndt said Chief Deputy Cotton and Sealy's Deputy Buck Childers, a full-blood Creek Indian, knew everybody in the county and people respected them. If someone was accused of a small crime, Cotton or Childers would telephone the offender, telling them to come on in, and they would. There was a saying about night calls though: "If Mr. Cotton has on his boots, you're all right, but if he's in his house shoes, look out, 'cause you done woke him up!"

Miss Pearl and Girndt told many funny and heart-warming stories, but terrible things happened at the jail, too. Billy George Hughs was one of them.

Officer Mark Henry had pulled over Hughs for an accusation of credit card theft, but Hughs shot Henry through the car window. When Hughs ended up on foot, Sheriff Maddox, Cotton Noviskie, and Buck Childers pursued with dogs. Girndt points out that unlike today, the dogs weren't trained to hold back on a prisoner once they caught him. The case could have easily been "closed" then and there. But these diligent officers restrained the dogs, arrested Hughs, and brought him back for trial.

Though convicted and sentenced for execution, Hughs played the court system for years, meanwhile running a radio program and a greeting card company from his Huntsville cell. He got a retrial after most of the key witnesses against him had passed away: Noviskie, Childers, and others. Despite that, a jury again gave him the death penalty.

The Austin County Jail had held other serious criminals before Hughs. At the very end of 1895, two separate murders occurred. Author Charles S. Fox of Houston details the event, complete with documents, in his book *The Double Hanging* (Bellville Historical Society, 1990), available at the museum.

After an argument, Clemons Strauther stole a gun, went to Alois Peter's house, and shot him. Strauther dropped the rifle and ran while Peter bled to death. When law officers confronted Strauther with the evidence and promised to protect him from lynching, Strauther surrendered and went to jail at Bellville. He was eventually sentenced to be hanged.

Shortly after that, Dora Emshoff, a widow, accompanied by her nine-year-old daughter, sold her cotton crop in Brenham. She started home, but a farmhand she recognized as Andrew Chappell stopped her, demanding her money. Chappell panicked and fired a shotgun, mortally wounding Mrs. Emshoff. When the horses bolted, Chappell fled. Somehow the little girl was able to steer the runaway team to a minister's home for help. Before Mrs. Emshoff died, she identified the man who had shot her, as did the child later on.

A tracking hound led Sheriff Dilmus Teague and his men to Chappell's home where they arrested him and took as evidence the recently fired shotgun. Sheriff Teague and his officers charged him with murder, but realizing the likelihood of a lynch mob, they took him to jail in Bellville by train. Over the next few days, the officers risked their own lives to thwart attempts by mobs and kept both Strauther and Chappell safe until sentiments cooled off. Chappell was tried and found guilty.

The double execution turned out to be a financial boon for Bellville when 2,000-3,000 men, women, and children showed up to witness the event. A photographer took orders for "before" and "after" pictures, both displayed at the museum. Officials built the scaffold in the woods, strung barbed wire around the area, and sold tickets. After Sheriff Glenn and Deputy Ed Chatham mounted the gallows with the two men, a minister gave a sermon and each prisoner made a speech.

Strauther again admitted his guilt, but Chappell continued to claim innocence. Then with hands and feet bound, black hoods pulled over their heads, and ropes adjusted, they stood face to face. Sheriff Glenn pushed the lever and the trapdoor dropped them. In nine to eleven minutes, a doctor pronounced both dead.

Author Charles Fox reports that after the prisoners were cut down, there were "the usual" morbid jokes and scramble to see the corpses, get a piece of the rope, and feel for heartbeats. Such was the scene of a typical public hanging of the times.

All is peaceful at the jail today, and the museum displays artifacts, relating not only to the jail and law enforcement, but also the area's role in Texas history. Still, I again felt a decided discomfort in the cell area. It's probably just as well they didn't turn the Austin County Jail into a bed and breakfast.

For information about visiting times or tours, contact the Austin County Jail Museum, 36 S. Bell, Bellville, TX 77418. (979) 865-5911 or visit their website at: www.austincounty.com/achc.html

*Austin County Jail current appearance.*

# Blanco
# Blanco County Jail
## (1877-1890)
## Historical Public Building

What would you do if you found a jail dating to 1877, one of the old-est buildings in town, partially buried, almost hidden inside anoth-er building, and robbed of its cell cage? Renee Benson, a local ranch owner, formed a company called "Uptown Blanco" and got to work. The old the-ater on the same block was what first got her attention regarding the need for restoration. In the process, she took on the task of renovating about ten other historical buildings as well.

To look at the magnificent courthouse, you'd have to wonder how such misfortunes could have happened to the jail. The town's courthouse, built in 1884, had a huge misfortune of its own. Its intended use lasted for only four years before the county was split, putting Blanco at one end of the county, instead of in the middle as required. Johnson City became the new county seat, and a courthouse was built there. One of the things the county fathers did was to remove the steel hardware from the old stone jail to use in a new jail in Johnson City.

Although early records are incomplete, at least one high profile killer had been incarcerated within the jail's walls. In 1885, while Blanco was still the county seat, a man named Al Lackey set out to exterminate his own family. He succeeded in killing six members, ranging from young to old, but was stopped before he managed to murder his wife and son. He was captured and thrown in jail, but a couple of days later a "necktie party" broke him out and lynched him in an oak tree. The tree still stands north of town on the west side of what is now Highway 281.

The jail originally faced the town square. It had four barred windows accessible by one metal-clad wooden door. The one room building had foot-and-a-half thick walls, secured with steel pins, and its interior dimensions were eighteen by twenty feet.

A general store almost as old as the jail, called the Comparet Building was built in front of the jail. After the old jail went out of service, about three feet of dirt filled the building when the poorly drained area was turned into an alley. Nevertheless, in 1994, the store added new walls and a concrete floor to connect the jail building, which customers could then enter at the rear of the store. It served as a barbershop and later part of a gift shop.

Since removing this connection and excavating the jail, the Uptown Blanco team has found an iron ring in the floor to which troublesome prisoners had been shackled.

And what of the other orphan, the courthouse? It has housed real estate brokers, lawyers, doctors, dentists, the justice of the peace, bankers, opera house audiences, hospital patients, students and numerous others. At one point, a buyer had planned to dismantle and move it to reconstruct as a home. But citizens organized The Old Blanco County Courthouse Preservation Society (OBCCPS), a private, non-profit corporation, and the group managed to block the deal.

Blanco citizens, it seems, are determined to preserve their history, whether it be a gigantic centerpiece or a tiny little almost forgotten jail. Renee Benson continues her beneficial efforts as owner and president of Renson Enterprises, Inc. and Uptown Blanco, LLC. She is also the founder and owner of Blanco Art Center, a multi-medium art school. Active in several civic and professional organizations, she also serves on the Board of Trustees for the University of the Incarnate Word in San Antonio.

For information about visiting times or tours, contact: Uptown Blanco, LLC., 503 3rd St., Blanco, TX 78606. (830) 833-1579

*Blanco County Jail current appearance.*

# Boerne
# Kendall County Jail
## (1884-1986)
## City and County offices

This chapter exemplifies the importance of historians. When records are lost or generations pass without recording the present, that era must either rely on hearsay or settle for oblivion. In the case of the Kendall County jails (yes, plural) at Boerne, their history might well have been salvaged through the fortunate coincidence that a history buff named John Eddie Vogt served as a deputy sheriff (1965-1968) and as a constable for about twenty years. It's little wonder that local people think of this as the first and only jail. It had been in use for 102 years before a newer jail replaced the old building in 1986.

Constantly working in and around the old buildings aroused Vogt's curiosity about some details that just didn't add up. On the same square with the stately courthouse are two sturdy rock buildings, the acknowledged 1884 jail and a smaller, one-story building behind it. Records state the latter was ordered to be converted into a grand jury room about the time the jail was finished. The question then becomes, what was the one-story building before it was converted? According to tradition it was called a pre-Civil War "commissary," but Vogt's research didn't agree with that. He began studying and transcribing courthouse records over 130 years old. The more research Vogt did, the more muddled the story became. He found references for the need of a new jail roof when the jail wasn't even finished yet, and an order to have "both" buildings whitewashed, which indicated another jail even before the "commissary."

Vogt, whose relatives went back to Boerne's formative years, pointed out still another small building up the street, which stories passed down through generations had referred to as a jail. The county had been organized during the Civil War in 1862. After the war, Reconstruction's mismanagement fostered lawlessness. For lawmen trying to maintain justice during this trying time there had to be a jail before 1884. One odd manifestation of the area involved gangs of white men that would rob, rape, and murder, then leave Indian paraphernalia to implicate native tribes.

Vogt noted evidence in the smaller "commissary" of where bars had been removed from the windows. He remembered that bars and metal bunks had been taken from one of the buildings to use in the nearby town of Comfort for a satellite jail (temporary holding when extra room is needed).

After much research, Vogt ran across a bill for "$5 to repair a *jail* window" in the courthouse—and the fact hit him. The wording for the 1870 building had called for "a courthouse and jail," not "a courthouse and *a* jail"! So the two had been housed under one roof, not an uncommon practice. The 1884 building, that most people called the first jail, is quite possibly the fourth, but despite much evidence, there is no absolute proof.

Instead of the usual living quarters for the sheriff, the bottom floor of this jail was made up of offices for the sheriff-tax assessor. The second floor cell area has room for another level of cells, but they were never needed. This area was remodeled in 1978, and the mostly two-bunk cells reflect the major prison reform movement of the 1970s.

Reflecting on his many years of public service, Vogt recalled an understanding between officers and a certain alcoholic. When going through periods of not trusting himself to be on the loose, the man simply admitted himself to "his" cell overnight, where he even had a coffee pot set up. The next morning he would go about his business in town.

Two cells stand isolated from the others and are designated for either women or juveniles. Vogt remembers a time when they had to arrest a mother for drunken behavior. It wasn't long before they got a call from dispatch about a disturbance. The detainees five or six children had all climbed the tree that grew next to their mother's cell window so they could talk to her.

When you visit the jail cell area, you'll notice a section of heavy mesh wire in the ceiling, put there to thwart escapes through the attic. Several instances led to this addition. One time a prisoner climbed down by way of sheets, but his impatient partner jumped and broke his leg. Two more serious escapes also occurred before steps were taken to secure the attic.

During Prohibition days, there was a well-known family in the county who were so proud of their bootleg whiskey that they actually labeled it. One of the family's several sons was arrested, but he escaped and crawled under the town's hotel (no longer there). He refused to come out, and Sheriff Bierschwale ended up having to shoot him.

Another escape happened the very first day Deputy John Eddie Vogt went on duty. A young serviceman named Gary had murdered his mother, brother, and nephew. Somehow he escaped from custody, and after a three-day manhunt, the sheriff's office got a call from the man's kinfolk saying that Gary was holed up in their barn. The law enforcement officers found him with a straight razor in his hand.

Sheriff Douglas Kuebel told Gary to lay down the razor, and he did, yielding to arrest without resistance. Gary was convicted and received three life sentences. The sheriff assigned Vogt and highway patrolman Joe Montgomery to take the prisoner to Huntsville. For meals, the lawmen removed one of Gary's handcuffs so he could eat, warning him that if he tried anything they would shoot him. The cashier chastised the officers for treating the poor boy so harshly. She may have felt differently after they told her his crime.

A few law-enforcement museum pieces have survived, one of which is a Thompson sub-machine gun. When the nearby gun factory closed, a Thompson family member gave the weapon to the Boerne sheriff's department. Who would have believed a "Tommy gun," usually associated with either war or the Mafia, would come into use in Boerne? But it did.

Sometimes prisoners who posed little danger of running away could do work around the building to earn a bit of extra food for lunch. One such prisoner, who had been cleaning the cells upstairs, saved a cupful of cleaner. The stairs up to the cells are narrow, and disappear around a corner. Sheriff Kuebel, taking food to the prisoner working upstairs, opened the cell door to hand in the food. Suddenly the prisoner threw the cleaner in the sheriff's eyes. Blinded and in agony, Kuebel staggered down the stairs and somehow managed to send a dispatch to Deputy Vogt for backup. Warning the prisoner what he was doing, Vogt stationed himself in a chair at the foot of the stairs and aimed the Tommy gun up the stairway. The prisoner stayed put and eventually gave up.

Fortunately Kuebel's sight returned after a couple of months. He was later killed in the line of duty after responding to a family disturbance. Used to being able to calm people down, Kuebel tried to reason with an enraged family member, but the guy fired a shotgun in the sheriff's direction, mortally wounding him. A marker honoring Sheriff Kuebel can be found in the Boerne town square.

When you visit this peaceful little town, such a violent past is hard to imagine. Rest assured it's safe to visit the old jail without incident as it was retired in 1986.

For information about arranging a tour, contact: County Offices—Historical Commission, P.O. Box 993, Boerne, TX 78006. Or call the Historical Commission at (830) 249-9343.

*Kendall County Jail current appearance.*

*McCulloch County Jail circa 1910. Courtesy of the Heart of Texas Historical Museum.*

# Brady
# McCulloch County Jail
## (1910-1975)
### Heart of Texas Historical Museum

The Heart of Texas Historical Museum found in Brady, Texas, gives a sense of what life was like for the town's residents through the years, and puts tourists on the scene by using different mediums. Museum board member Bert Streigler, and his wife gave my husband and me a tour of the facility. Annette Williamson, daughter of Sheriff J.P. Williamson, wrote and illustrated a story/coloring book (available for purchase) from her viewpoint as a six-year-old in 1951.

Children can relate to "Pigtail Annie's" mischievous stories of growing up in the jail, which looks like "the sheriff's castle." She quotes her father explaining to her about the prisoners, "The people I must put upstairs . . . for some reason . . . do wrong things . . . that might hurt other people and themselves."

Museum volunteers have made video interviews of noteworthy towns-people, such as former Sheriff Luke Vogel, ninety years old at the time. He and his wife were the last to serve in the jail before it closed in 1975. It is a treat to hear the stories from the man himself, as if he were walking around the building with you.

Impressive paintings hang on the wall, and I was particularly taken with two that showed frontiersmen on horseback: one labeled Ben McCulloch, hero of the Texas Revolution (after whom the county is named), and the other, Peter Brady (after whom the town is named). Both were Texas Rangers. As it turns out, the latter was the great, great grandfather of the artist who created and donated the paintings, Frederick Hambly of Arizona.

The building itself is attractive and well kept, and Striegler explained the similar look of many jails. At least thirty-eight in Texas alone were made by the same manufacturer, Southern Structural Steel Company of San Antonio. The cells and other structures would arrive prefabricated via railroad flatcars. The steel cages were assembled on the site and welded together. The walls went up around the metal casings.

The kitchen is renovated to its original appearance, down to the kitchen sink. When word went out about the renovation, a citizen who had salvaged the first sink brought it back. Townspeople contributed appropriate furniture and household items to make the room look as if the wife of the first sheriff might enter any moment and begin preparing a meal for her family and a jail full of prisoners.

Displays are arranged by themes. One particular exhibit from the World War II collection relates a series of events that would make a great true adventure book or documentary. The short version is that Houston Braley, a young pilot from Brady, was flying his plane low to strafe a German train in France, when an explosion caused him to crash into a cathedral. French townspeople took Braley's body where the Germans couldn't find it. Many years later, Braley's squadron paid tribute to the heroes of the village by collecting enough money to replace the windows in the cathedral. Since then, tour groups from France have visited the Brady Museum where this entire story with photos is commemorated.

A German World War II veteran visited the exhibit some years later. During the war the man had been a prisoner in the German POW camp located about three miles out of Brady. His sons, who had become American citizens and served in the U.S. Air Force, brought him back to the area to visit the museum. Talking through a translator, the man contributed his collection of photos and memorabilia relating to the prison camp.

While we can't visit with those bygone soldiers, Sheriff Luke Vogel tells us in his videotape about what it was like for him and his wife Verna during the last years that the building was used as a jail. When Vogel left ranching to keep the peace, he had to pay for his own social security and insurance. A sheriff was also expected to pay for guns and handcuffs. The garage that came with the sheriff's apartment should have been a perk, but the one in Brady was built for a Model T, and Vogel's "modern" car wouldn't fit, so they turned the garage into a washroom (it took a hail storm damaging the car to convince the county to build a carport). One would think that a sheriff's office would be an unquestioned part of the building, but when Vogel asked for one, the county commissioners said, "You want an office, build it yourself." Vogel had to explain the importance of a separate room with a steel door through which prisoners would be brought in. In this room, the sheriff would book the prisoner and deliver a "lecture." After much prodding, the room was built. Today visitors can see that the ceiling opens to the never used hanging gallows, with the trapdoor above still visible.

The food and medicine allowance for each prisoner was $1.20 per day, later going up to $1.50, but the Vogels supplemented this from their own pockets. They fed the prisoners the same meals they themselves ate, and prisoners who proved they could be trusted were brought down to the dining room to eat with the family.

Twenty-seven prisoners were the most they ever had at one time, and the cells were empty on only two occasions. With thirty-eight windows, prisoners suffered terrible mosquito bites, so Vogel convinced the county officers to put screens on the windows because, as he said, "These boys look like they've got the chicken pox."

Most prisoners responded to Vogel's fair but no-nonsense treatment, and those who were convicted of a crime punishable by prison time often left their valuables in the sheriff's care before they went, saying, "I'd never get it back there."

The drunk tank was on the third floor, and some of the overnight guests had to sleep on a mattress on the floor for fear they would fall off a narrow bunk. Vogel told Streigler he'd like to strangle the jail designer for putting the drunk tank up there. "I've had to put many a drunk cowboy over my shoulder and carry him up. Later, after I got the bright idea to open that trapdoor and let the noose hang down where they saw it, most of them were able to walk up by themselves."

Vogel only had to pull his gun once during an arrest. He and a deputy were breaking up a fight, and the participants needed some extra persuasion to stop. Fortunately, Vogel didn't have to use the drawn weapon. Only one prisoner kept giving Vogel trouble, and the convict spent time in the jail at least twice before being sent to the "pen." This incorrigible broke pipes, "cussed" the sheriff, and tried to tempt him to violence. Wisely Sheriff Vogel didn't leave himself open for abuse charges. On a couple of occasions outside, he offered this guy a chance to fight him fairly, only to get the answer, "I'm smarter than that. You'd whup me."

Not only men came through McCulloch County Jail. Once a young woman who had killed a man spent time there until transferred to Huntsville. Another time, a man and his wife shared a cell.

Only one prisoner ever escaped. A locksmith by trade, the escapee made several keys that broke when he tried to use them. When his talents failed the man found a nail and scraped out mortar to remove bricks. He left by way of the roof and then stole a car and lit out for Abilene. One day later, he was shot and killed for cheating in a card game.

The museum board is constantly improving the site and has plans underway to add other structures, such as buildings from the POW camp, to make an entire historical complex. The jail museum is located a block west of the square.

For information about visiting times or tours, contact: Heart of Texas Historical Museum, P.O. Box 1401, Brady, TX 76825-1401. (325) 597-0526 or visit their website at: www.bradytx.com/sites3/museum.html

*McCulloch County Jail architectural detail (current appearance).*

*McCulloch County Jail current appearance.*

*Brown County Jail circa 1905. Courtesy of Brown County Museum of History.*

## Brownwood
# Brown County Jail
## (1903-1981)
### Brown County Museum of History

The history of the Brown County Jail has a certain flair about it, with some incidents downright theatrical. But then what would one expect on seeing a towering medieval castle in the middle of town? Two earlier jails preceded the unique structure, one of which burned, so the townspeople pulled out all the stops on the one built in 1903, making the building four stories high with a basement to boot.

Having learned their lesson about fires, the builders only used lumber for interior walls in the first floor sheriff's quarters. The three floors above the sheriff's quarters were built of nothing but native sandstone, cement, and steel. Each eighteen by eighteen inch block was hand-chiseled to fit varying lengths, some as long as six feet. This must have presented manual laborers quite a challenge, and it took eight or ten mules to pull the heavy wagons from the quarry. Builders were paid a dollar for each ten-hour day, six days a week.

When finished, the sheriff's apartment was a show place, but inmates' cells were definitely no frills, and each floor up grew progressively more stark. The building held as many as ninety prisoners at one time. The nicest perk that lower level offenders housed on the second floor had was time out of their four-man cells in the "bull pen," a large open cage in the middle of the floor. On Sundays, their friends and family could stand around it to visit and even bring tobacco and food treats.

The third floor housed more violent prisoners in higher-security cells, and the only way out was for a law officer to open the doors. The gallows and trapdoor were also installed, but no hanging ever took place.

The fourth floor held the worst prisoners of all—in solitary confinement.

Even in the 1930s, a deputy's children who lived in the first floor apartment remembered no electric lights or heating in the cells. Inmates were given a cardboard fan for summer cooling. Thanksgiving and Christmas dinners were the only departure from the everyday beans, bread, and corn or potatoes. Meals were hauled up to the cells through a dumbwaiter.

Much of the information shared with me by the Brown County Historical Society came from Lorene Bishop's weekly column, "Scrapbook," published in the *Brownwood Bulletin*. One such column covered a 1988 speech to the Historical Society, delivered by Sheriff Donohoo. He said of the frontier sheriffs, "Everybody ended up being shot." During one dispute, Sheriff Harris killed former Sheriff Roberts, and was then shot by a school teacher. During an arrest in 1897, Sheriff Bell was killed. His deputy killed the man; then was killed himself in another raid.

The most infamous shooting involved John Wesley Hardin. One version of the story has it that Deputy Charlie Webb had tracked Hardin down and confronted him. Hardin killed Deputy Webb and got away. Furious, a posse gave chase, and when they couldn't find Hardin, they hanged three of his men and his brother instead. Although the brother had not been involved, the posse reasoned that, since he was a lawyer and might eventually defend John Wesley, he should be hanged as a preventative measure.

In fact, Hardin was later found and convicted, earning a twenty-five year prison sentence for shooting Deputy Webb. He used his prison time to "read the law," and when he received a pardon, he practiced law. His "fame" caught up with him in El Paso when a wannabe gunslinger shot him in the back.

Escapes played a part in the jail's history, two of them during the terms of the jails first sheriff. Sheriff Mose Denman, first elected in 1900, didn't take kindly to it when a cattle thief escaped, so when the fugitive was apprehended in Tombstone, Arizona, Sheriff Denman went after him. To his chagrin, a legality in Arizona prevented Denman from taking the prisoner back, but he didn't let that stop him. He kidnapped the prisoner and left by a different route, through the desert. Both sheriff and prisoner almost died of thirst, but at last made it back to Brownwood.

Sheriff's wives did their part, too. One day the milkman asked Mrs. Denman if she was hanging sheets from the upper windows to dry. When she went to check, she found that two prisoners had cut through the bars and shinnied down the sheets.

One Sunday morning, Sheriff Townsend (1961-1971) went to church, leaving his wife sick in bed. She heard someone trying to get through her door, and knowing the jailer was upstairs tending the prisoners, she called out. The intruder ran away, apparently startled to find someone home. About that time, she heard the jailer rattling a cell door and calling for help. A prisoner had managed to steal the jailer's keys and trade places with him.

The adage, "Truth is stranger than fiction," proves its point in the 1970 case of prisoner Rae Bourbon, a female impersonator who claimed to have performed for or worked with about every celebrity alive. During one of his traveling tours, Bourbon had left his seventy dogs, five cats, and two skunks in an animal shelter. On returning and getting his pet boarding bill, Bourbon contested it hotly. He ended up killing the owner, which landed Bourbon in the Brown County Jail. While there, he got permission from the jailer to make a phone call. When he finished his call, Bourbon couldn't find the jailer, but he did find an open door. Stories differ after that point. One says Bourbon was afraid the law enforcement officers would shoot him so he turned himself in. Another version says he sat down waiting to be shot in hopes of "ending it all" since he was quite ill. The law officers brought him back to jail instead.

The last jailbreak came four years after the facility had closed in 1981. An article appeared in *Brownwood Bulletin*, titled, "Teen Finally Breaks out of Jail." A fourteen year old boy, taking a regular tour, departed for the then-off-limits upper floor. He entered the cell directly under the tower and slammed the door behind him. What he didn't know was that nobody had a key to that cell! The fire department had to use their aerial ladder to climb on the roof. The gallows trapdoor at last came into use when they were able to lift the lad through it to freedom.

In case you want more evidence of the theatrics involving the Brown County Jail, consider the communication from the Camden, New Jersey Chief of Police in 1921. The chief had received a letter from eight prisoners, claiming to be hard-working cowboys on a Texas ranch. The letter stated that the "cowboys" wanted to correspond with nice girls "with a view of matrimony." The piece does not say whether these lonely Texas boys got any takers.

The old jail, maintained by the Brown County Museum of History and the Historical Commission, can be found at 212 N. Broadway, diagonally across from the courthouse square. For information about visiting times or tours, contact: the Brown County Museum of History, P.O. Box 2006, Brownwood, TX 76804-2006. (325) 641-1926 or visit their website at: www.browncountyhistory.org

*Brown County Jail current appearance. Stacey Hasbrook photographer.*

# Buffalo Gap
# Taylor County
# Courthouse-Jail
## (1879-1883)
### Buffalo Gap Historic Village

Citizens of Buffalo Gap built the large stone courthouse-jail to serve Taylor County forever. Rows of cannon balls were sandwiched between the large stone blocks in spaces hollowed out for them. This not only held the walls straight, but also thwarted the efforts of any prisoner who tried to escape by scraping out the mortar to loosen the stones. The ground floor contained county offices as well as a courtroom.

Sad to say, the town held its county seat status only from 1878-1883, with this original building constructed in 1879. Blessed with tall trees and abundant ground water, Buffalo Gap occupies a point in the Callahan Divide that cuts through to the flat lands—an oasis before the plains. For hundreds of years, buffalo had beaten a trail followed later by cattle drives. Why would such a place be virtually abandoned? Because the railroad bypassed it. When tracks were laid east to west through the new town of Abilene a few miles to the north, the county seat went there too. The citizens of Buffalo Gap were not happy about the decision to move the county seat to Abilene, and when they learned that one of their own judges voted against keeping the county seat in Buffalo Gap, they took their revenge by enjoying a fried chicken picnic with the judge's chickens.

For those few short years, prisoners from "the wild town of Abilene" were incarcerated here. One large room or runabout held the common criminals and drunks while a single corner cell at the head of the stairs was reserved for incorrigibles. Plastered stone makes up three sides with one high, narrow window allowing scant daylight and ventilation. Its boilerplate steel wall has a barred door with a padlock.

After this jail was no longer needed, a family lived on the second floor. Thanks to historians Ernest Wilson and Dr. R. Lee Rode, who owned the structure at different times beginning in 1956, not just the old Taylor County Courthouse-Jail was saved, but other buildings were brought in as well. The only structure older than the courthouse at the Historic Village is the 1875 log cabin, formerly the home of a buffalo hunter. A charming little 1881 cottage, home to Abilene's first marshal John Thomas Hill, was also moved in to sit only a few feet from the courthouse-jail. Marshal Hill, shot in the toe during an altercation, later died of complications. His funeral took place in the house, and possibly that of his wife and daughter, who lived out their lives and also died there.

In 1999, the Grady McWhiney Research Foundation, affiliated with McMurry University, bought the Village to be further developed and operated as an educational facility. The Buffalo Gap Historic Village has collected about twenty vintage buildings, each one fully furnished according to its appropriate era, and represents the last fifty years of the Old West. Enclosed inside a fence in the middle of Buffalo Gap, Texas history is not only saved, but shared with all who come to visit, and the staff provides not only static displays but special events with living history interpretations.

As you meander along the trails among chickens, cats, and old fashioned gardens, you almost expect to meet the original inhabitants. In fact, many visitors claim they have! Former site manager Justin Frazier said that something at the Hill House seems to especially like young men: "Our college boys that work out there are the ones that have 'events:' banging screen doors, motion past windows, etc. Dogs, too, find the house a little daunting, and will often bark at unseen things."

Throughout the Village, recorded sounds add to the mood such as a Victrola playing music in the parlor of the marshal's house and distant sounds of trains at the railroad depot. Sound wands that provide in-depth explanations about artifacts and the area's history are now available as well. People compliment the staff on these details, plus other sounds they can't account for. The second floor jail runabout houses a collection of guns and Indian artifacts. As for the cell reserved for incorrigibles, I could find no records of who they were. However, kids who are visiting ask from time to time, "Who's the guy in the jail cell?" That cell stays locked, and there's nobody there.

The town of Buffalo Gap lies about eight miles south of Abilene on Highway 89, otherwise known as Buffalo Gap Road. The Village is located at the corner of Elm and Williams Streets. For information about the educational programs, visiting times or tours, contact: (325) 572-3365 or visit their website at: www.buffalogap.com

Author's note: I attended a nighttime investigation of the Buffalo Gap Historic Village with a team of so-called "ghost hunters." Alternate chapters about this and three other Texas jails (Bandera, Gonzales, and Lockhart) are included in the anthology *Ghostly Tales from America's Jails* (Atriad Press, 2003).

*Taylor County Courthouse-Jail current appearance. Courtesy of Buffalo Gap Historic Village.*

*Hammond House circa 1900s. Courtesy of Bill Hammond Norton.*

## Calvert
# Robertson County Jail
## (1870-1881)
## Hammond House B&B

To look at the stately Hammond House, you'd never believe what a hard time it's had trying to serve a purpose. It's coming close to having as many lives as a cat. To begin with, in 1870 during the confused days of Reconstruction, the state legislature proclaimed Calvert, Texas, as seat of Robertson County. That three other towns had been named before, and the legislature had changed its mind was not auspicious. In an effort to seal the deal, Calvert hastened to build an awe-inspiring jail and made plans to add a courthouse close by as soon as possible. True to form, a mere nine years later, the county seat was again moved, this time to Franklin. The steel cells were gutted from this building, and hauled to the latest choice. And though the sign out front for years erroneously called this building the courthouse, none was ever built.

Andy Faulkner bought it and turned it into a hotel, partitioning the empty cell area with regular walls to accommodate a new kind of clientele.

In 1885 he sold it to Robert Brown, who made it a residence, but only until 1909, when he sold it to Fannie Lee Hammond. Fannie Lee used the bottom floor for the family home and rented the upstairs to boarders. Bustling railroad business no doubt provided plenty of takers. One of her children, as an adult, continued the business, and also brought up a family there. When Mr. Hammond died in the house in 1963, his heirs sold it to the Calvert Chamber of Commerce. They deeded it to the Robertson County Historical Society to turn into a museum, but that organization had more than it could handle and eventually decided to deed it back to the family.

Enter Bill Norton, great grandson of Fannie Lee Hammond, whose father had grown up in the house. He was the only one of the heirs who wanted the building, and in 1995 he undertook the job of personally restoring the structure, a project that would occupy him for almost a dozen years. All the while, he was living in Austin and holding a full-time job. Don and I first met Norton in the old building that he'd stripped down mostly to the original bricks. In the process, he's become an expert on many subjects: town history, original jail blueprints, and grant applications, to name a few.

The Texas Historical Commission dubbed Hammond House an "Endangered Historic Property of Texas," and Norton's first priorities were to stop the "rising damp" that was eating away the bricks from the bottom and a leaky roof eating it from the top. The most unfortunate and nearly disastrous thing that happened to the building came shortly before Norton inherited it. Some well-intentioned people during the museum days took out the wood floors and poured in a concrete slab, but with no water barriers. To make matters worse, they also installed sheet rock, further taking away the chance for the lower structural masonry to ever dry out. After much trenching and brick replacement, the building was once more sound.

As a jail, it had not included a full second floor. Instead the cell area had two tiers of cells stacked one on top of the other, rising a story and a half high. The only stairs had been wrought iron leading to the upper level balcony and cells. Two rooms on that level had evidently served the sheriff and/or jailer. Separate cells were provided for women and the insane, though whether both occupied the space together we don't know. Of course Norton never saw these cages and cells, since they had been moved to the subsequent county jail, but he did have the blueprints. Also while sorting out which stage was which, he said at least he could tell the oldest part by the use of square nails.

He has photos of the project on his website, including the charming finished rooms. Several elaborate fireplace mantels and bathtubs of various sizes and shapes are relics of hotel and boarding house days. And when Robert Brown made it home-sweet-home, he added a charming bay window area. A carriage house stands nearby too, added during hotel days to provide a kitchen and manager's room.

For information contact: Bill Hammond Norton, 8820 Mountain Path Circle, Austin, TX 78759. (512) 680-0978, bnorton@austin.rr.com or visit their website at: www.thehammondhouse.com

*Hammond House current appearance.*

# Cameron
# Milam County Jail
## (1895-1975)
### Milam County Historical Jail Museum

When you come into Cameron on Highway 77, headed northwest, you may be startled to see a castle taller than the trees to your left. This castle, actually the old Milam County Jail, is diagonally across from the courthouse square. Just as awesome up close, its red brick is accented by white limestone window arches and keystones at the base of each corner turret. Look closely and you'll see that the carved design on each is different: handcuffs, grapes, ivy, and my favorite, a wolf. The tower rises five floors high to the gallows, but no one was ever hanged—there. Museum Director Charles King says as far as records show, the only hanging that took place inside the jail was self-inflicted by a prisoner in his cell.

Of the two front doors, one leads into the sheriff's family quarters, but visitors enter where prisoners used to say goodbye to freedom. The sheriff's office is visible through a small window on your right. Notice the thick walls with steel doors. This small space was the only part of the first floor accessible to a prisoner. From there, the incarcerated was conducted past a huge boiler that heated the building and up the steel spiral stairs to his cell. To accommodate modern visitors, however, newer and less hazardous stairs have been installed in what used to be a bedroom of the sheriff's quarters.

The rest of the first floor shows how the sheriff's home may have looked with impressive antique furnishings. Even the tables are set as if the family might sit down to dinner at any time. Many of the items on display have historic significance, and a few mannequins model Victorian clothing.

In the cells of the second through fourth floors, a couple of not-so-well-dressed mannequins wait. King says he can always tell by the kids' delighted squeals when they happen on these surprise "inmates." They also like getting locked in cells when he demonstrates the remote locking system. An entertaining guide, he thrives on group tours. King says some groups, including a classic car club, make annual trips here. Schools in Cameron and nearby Rockdale bring students of a certain grade each year on a history field trip, so that in the long run, all get their turns. While teaching history, King provides a sense of fun so his visitors will want to come back on their own.

People often ask two kinds of questions about a jail: Are there are any ghosts? And any stories about the good guys and the bad guys? About the first question, King answers that some kids have reported stories about ghosts, but nothing specific. For his own part and that of museum volunteers, they periodically smell body odor at one place in the kitchen, but that's all.

About the second question, he could probably go on all day, but here are a few anecdotes.

Milam County's first jail was as humble as this one is elegant, and like most jails of its kind, it is long gone. It consisted merely of a log cabin built over a dungeon (see Gatesville chapter for a similar surviving example). At least one successful jail break took place there when a woman came to visit her inmate husband. Just as the jailer opened the trapdoor to let her husband come out, the wife threw her cloak over the jailer. During the scuffle that allowed the man to escape, the woman's hand was crushed in the trapdoor. The ungrateful husband rode away on the horse she had brought for him, never to return. She was left to make her living as a seamstress, handicapped by a crippled hand.

When the new jail was built, materials and artisans, such as stone and brick masons, arrived by train, and the site was handy to the tracks. The second through fourth floors provided cells for forty-five inmates. Once these inmates arrived they served work details on a prison farm and were hauled to and from work by wagon. Cow horns, on display at the museum, were used to call the crews back to home-sweet-jail.

King pointed out a small hole in the ceiling of the first floor. It was above the place where a case of Coca-Cola™ soft drinks had once been stored behind the metal lockup door. A couple of prisoners in a second-floor cell had chiseled out a hole through which they could lower a looped string and lasso Coke bottles one at a time to pull up through the hole.

Also on display is law enforcement memorabilia. Deputy Sheriff Greg Kuba researched and commemorated all sheriffs who have served Milam County. One of these was Sheriff Sara White (1942-1945), the first woman sheriff of the county and only the fourth in Texas. Like other women who took "men's" jobs during World War II, Sara accepted the position when her husband, second term sheriff Valter White, was inducted into the military service. Citizens remembered her as a sheriff who "pinned her badge to her dress, carried a pistol in her purse, and conducted business in a stern manner," according to the information on one website.

She apparently continued to work from her office, while the same chief deputy who served under her husband made arrests, etc. This officer, Carl Black, went on to succeed her as sheriff. Elected in 1944, he held that office for thirty-two years, the longest tenure in the county's history.

Both as a deputy and as a sheriff, he left a legacy of stories that show the respect he inspired for being a big man both in character and physical size. Once during a shoot-out, several officers were in a stand-off behind their cars while a group of young men were holed up in a house. Sheriff Black went to the door, ripped it off its hinges, and arrested the outlaws. Another time, prisoners had dug through the outer jail wall and shinnied down the rain spout. When they met Sheriff Black waiting for them with a shotgun, they climbed back up the pipe. These are only a few of the stories you'd hear if the old jail could talk.

Another interesting feature to the site at the log cabin that belonged to a circuit-riding preacher named Joseph Sneed. The full story is in the museum brochure, but the barn (original to the site), houses antique farm machinery.

When historical collections outgrew the walls of the jail-museum, officials expanded to a Museum Annex one block away on Main Street. Exhibits, beautifully displayed in glass cases, range from the Batte doll collection, to Civil War letters, to Spanish missions, to machinery, to Texas Ranger memorabilia. Not encased is a row of old typewriters and Morse-code telegraphs on a lower shelf, an invitation for kids to try them out. King says children love to get their hands on anything with working parts, and if you want young people to come away with pleasant impressions of museums, you need more than "Do not touch" messages.

As you leave the Museum Annex, watch for murals on the outside walls of the buildings around town. My favorite is on Travis Street, left from Main as you drive west from the square. Realistically painted Texas Rangers line up on horseback across the wall, and if it looks familiar, it's because you saw the historical photograph, from which it was copied, in the museum.

For information about visiting times or tours, contact: Milam County Historical Museum, P.O. Box 966, Cameron, TX 76520. (254) 697-4979

For more information about Sheriff Sara White, visit: www.ancestorhunt.com/historic-sheriffs.htm

*The Milam County Jail has different carvings on each keystone, such as this wolf.*

*Milam County Jail current appearance.*

*Panola County Jail. Photo courtesy of Panola County Historical and Genealogical Association.*

# Carthage
# Panola County Jail
## (1891-1953)
## La Grone Family History Center
## and Museum

If you live in Carthage, you can expect to find your relatives in jail—records of them, that is, at the Family History Center of the Panola County Jail Museum. But how did a jail come into this role? It started off like most jails, housing prisoners for seventy-four years. It had a sheriff's office and a four-room home for the jailer, whose wife cooked for the inmates. The second floor had four, four-man cells, with "bean holes" for tin plates and cups to be passed through. The whole building was heated by potbellied stoves.

Built in 1891, the structure, known locally as "Old Red" for its brick, is the oldest surviving building in town. Its top commands attention, and it served the county until a new facility replaced it in 1953. Even after the city bought the building, it continued as a city jail for a dozen more years. When it quit being a jail, the Carthage Book Club leased it for a while and turned it into a historical museum.

For many years after that, it stood deserted, prey to vandals and the elements, even though the Panola Bicentennial Commission of 1976 got it registered as a National Historic Shrine. No interested group had the funds to replace the rotting floor or roof, and only one of its iron doors was left. Even when the City and the newly organized Panola County Historical and Genealogical Association (PCHGA) agreed to take on restoration of the jail as a place for their museum and family history library, no one knew where they would get the $96,000 an architect told them it would take to renovate the old building.

City and county officials put their heads together with a retired school teacher named Leila LaGrone, who was already well known for the several books she had written about area history, such as the *Regulator-Moderator War*. She also gave radio and television broadcasts on the subject of local heritage. Under her leadership, the PCHGA was able to obtain a small grant and to inspire countless small private donations. One thing members did was a rocking chair event they called "Jailhouse Rock," that brought in $3,000. Another was their publication of *The History of Panola County*, which garnered $16,000.

In 1991, the project was completed for two-thirds the estimated cost. LaGrone (at age eighty-two) said, "We have done much of the work ourselves as volunteers, . . . and had a big blow-out . . . " This blow-out brought Gov. Ann Richards and a bevy of other state and local dignitaries to help the PCHGA celebrate Old Red's hundredth birthday. Fittingly, the name of the library is the "Leila Belle LaGrone Family History Center."

Since then, the Center has continued to collect genealogy books and documents, and the library has created museum exhibits. Upon entering the building, visitors see a collection of paintings by Q.M. Martin, as well as his personal memorabilia. Besides being an artist, this innovative superintendent of Carthage schools had been the driving force behind the establishment of Panola College, which in turn honored him by naming an auditorium after him.

On the second floor, cell space is utilized to pay tribute to past law enforcement and fire department officials, with one cell still holding a mannequin prisoner. There's also a pioneer section and a Veterans Memorial that includes a scale model of the *Via Panola Express,* a World War II plane named for the county.

"Old Red" has made a home to something else unique: the East Texas Oral History Archives, collected by students of both Carthage High School and Panola College. Hundreds of interviews include cassette tapes and typed transcripts on such topics as The Great Depression, three wars, church history, Panola College, and family recollections. Ann Morris began the collection in 1986, which continues to grow, along with those collected from Professor Joe Hough of Panola College.

A plaque outside the jail reads: ". . . Twelve Panola County sheriffs have served as custodian of the jail; used as residence by some, and child of one born in jail."

For information about visiting times or tours, contact: The Old Panola County Jail, 211 N. Shelby St., Carthage, TX 75633. (903) 693-3388 or visit their website at: www.carthagetexas.com/historical/1891jail.htm

*Portable Jail for chain gang prisoners.*
*Courtesy of Grayson County Frontier Village.*

# Denison
# Grayson County's
# Two Extremely Rare Jails
## Portable Jail (ca. 1877-1930)
## at Frontier Village

Grayson County was home to not one but two extremely rare jails, and they couldn't have been more opposite: from the most humble to the most elaborate "high-tech" of the age.

You might call the portable jail the forerunner to a modern recreation vehicle (sans recreation). It could sleep thirty men, and in it prisoners were hauled to a job site to maintain roads. Yes, that photo of a strap-iron cell on wheels is what I'm talking about, and believe it or not, a wooden platform halfway up made a second floor. As Frontier Village board member John Crawford remarked, "It wasn't the Hilton."

What heinous crime could warrant such punishment? Vagrancy. The Civil War and Reconstruction period left droves of people homeless and jobless. County judge and historian J.N. Dickson explained the situation in his writings. After Reconstruction finally ended and the Texas State

Constitution had been adopted, a vagrancy law was enacted in 1876 in response to the unemployment problem. At least on the chain gang there was employment, and bed and board with amenities: straw padding and one oversized blanket for the inmates on each floor to share. In case of rain or snow, the guards would roll down a curtain to protect the prisoners from the elements. Judge Dickson remembers that convicts generally made the best of things, often times creating their own music in camp at night.

Considering the number of vagrants arrested, it's not hard to understand that incarcerating all of them in the Grayson County Jail at Sherman was impossible. Putting able-bodied men on the chain gang only made sense. The judge also wrote that besides the two prisoner wagons, there had been cabins on wheels built for the foreman and guards, and wagons that hauled tools and supplies. John Crawford has combined Judge Dickson's articles into a booklet, which can be obtained at the Frontier Village.

The portable jail wagons were in use until the vagrancy law was repealed in 1929—just before the Great Depression when unemployment again became a huge problem.

## Grayson County Jail at Sherman (1887-1930) (now gone)

A nd what about that "high-tech" county jail, the chain gang stayed in when not on the move? Visualize a rotary cell block. Patented in 1881 by William Brown and Benjamin Haugh of Indianapolis, it was designed to provide maximum security with minimum jailer attention. This unique jailhouse was a marvel of engineering. Prisoners were housed in the circular part of the facility, which consisted of a drum divided into about ten pie-shaped cells on each floor, and the photo shows two floors. The drum rotated by a hand-turned crank lined up only one cell at a time with a single doorway. Other parts of the building had offices, living quarters for sheriff or jailer, a kitchen, and trustee cells.

Only three rotary jails remain intact in America, and they are immensely popular as tourist attractions. The largest, with three tiers of cells, is in Council Bluffs, Iowa. This "Squirrel Cage" jail served as the Pottawattamie County Jail from 1885 to 1969. Historian Ryan Roenfeld states on the

Squirrel Cage website, "A total of eighteen rotary jails are thought to have been built altogether around the country, but details remain sketchy. The majority . . . contained two tiers of cells and were constructed by the Pauly Jail Building and Manufacturing Company of Saint Louis, Missouri. Today, only three remain [with cells intact] and all are open to the public as museums showcasing one of Americas more peculiar methods of penal incarceration." (www.thehistoricalsociety.org/Jail.htm)

Of the eighteen, two were in Texas: the Ellis County Jail (1888) in Waxahachie, which is still standing, but all the rotary "works" have been gutted (see "Jails Waiting" section); and the Grayson County Jail (1877) in Sherman, which was obliterated.

This amazing building served for sixty-three years and may have continued except for one grim event in the county's history. On a day in 1930, a black man, accused of raping a white woman, was escorted to the courthouse for his trial. A mob became so enraged that officials locked the prisoner inside the walk-in vault for safe keeping. Even a company of Texas Rangers couldn't calm the ensuing riot. The mob blasted a hole in the courthouse, set it on fire, and then extracted the prisoner. Even though the man was already dead, they hanged him from a tree and burned his body. Still not satisfied, they went on to burn businesses owned by other African-Americans.

R.C. Vaughan, who is now a retired district judge and also a past board president for Frontier Village, remembers as a teenager, watching the conflagration from a distance.

The rotary jail was razed as soon as a new jail was built on the top floor of the new courthouse. Anyone who wants to see how a rotary cell jail works will have to go to Council Bluffs, Iowa—or at least look at the photos and model on the previously named website. However, one relic of the Grayson County Jail was saved. About the time it was demolished, the Civilian Conservation Corps (CCC) of the Depression era was building Loy Park in Denison where Frontier Village is located. Half the circular rail from the jail's rotating system was brought there.

Today one portable jail wagon remains in Frontier Village, an 1800s town made up of fifteen original buildings and museum. The park is located at Denison, Highway 75 South and Loy Lake Road (Exit 67). When you enter the park notice the half circle iron rail, now with lights added, that makes the entranceway a reminder of the lost rotary cell jail building.

For information about visiting times or tours, contact: Frontier Village, P.O. Box 646, Denison, TX 75021, (903) 463-2487 or visit their website at: www.rootsweb.com/~txgrayso/frontierv.html

*One of eighteen rotary-cell jails in the nation, built in 1877. Now gone.*
*Courtesy of Grayson County Frontier Village.*

*Last vestige of rare 1877 county jail, the iron rail.*
*Courtesy of Grayson County Frontier Village.*

*Hidalgo County Jail circa 1910. Courtesy of the Museum of South Texas History.*

## Edinburg
# Hidalgo County Jail
## (1910-1922)
### Museum of South Texas History

The very name "Hidalgo" (nobleman) conjures visions of landed gentry, especially in the lush, subtropical climate of extreme South Texas, and well it should. In the early 1800s, Salomé Balli inherited the land grant her ranching great-grandfather had received from Spain. The city names later given to this land, "Edinburg" and "McAllen," seem puzzling, but can be explained. Señorita Balli married a Brownsville businessman named John Young about 1848. After he died, she eventually married her late husband's associate, John McAllen. Both men had increased their land holdings through the years.

Meanwhile, the new Hidalgo county seat (moved from Old Hidalgo) had been named after a Mr. Chapin, but in 1911, when he was involved in a murder trial, the citizens nixed the name. Instead they wanted to honor respectable men, Young and McAllen, so in reference to their birthplace in Scotland, the name "Edinburg" (with the "h" dropped) was selected. Also the city just to the south was dubbed "McAllen."

True to form, the earliest public buildings to go up were a jail and a courthouse, completed in 1910. The jail's Spanish Mission Revival design made it an object of respect. It had a clay tile roof with walls and tower made of solid brick. Wood burning stoves were used for heating, and for water there was a windmill and wooden holding tank.

When visitors enter what used to be the sheriff's or jailer's office, they can still look up and see the steel trapdoor of the gallows. A set of stairs once ascended from the office so that the jailer could escort prisoners directly to the jail area. Later adaptations of the building needed the space for something else, and the stairs were moved to another location. The jailer's living quarters occupied the rest of the first floor.

Upstairs is a large room that once contained steel cell blocks, but they were removed at some point. Two other small, closed-in rooms remain. The "violent cell," for solitary confinement has a solid steel door with a small "peep hole" for the jailer to open when he wanted to check or converse with the prisoner. Inside is an old bed and mattress, but Education Director Judy McClelland explains to kids, "It was more likely that the mattress was the only furniture the unruly prisoner was given." The other small room has a barred door on it, and it opens into the hanging room.

For his crime of rape and murder in 1913, a convicted man paid the price at the end of a rope on that gallows. Archivist Esteban Lomas says that is the only documented execution in the jail. Nevertheless, rumors of two suicides in the cells come up from time to time. And some swear to having heard shackles clanking and other sounds from the old jail in the night.

When a newer, larger jail was built in 1922, the old jail was used for a community center for a time, then converted to a fire station and city hall in the 1930s. A garage for the fire trucks stood in the present Heritage Courtyard. Firemen bunked on the second floor and slid down a pole to the garage.

In June 2006, the museum hosted Shorty Bishop, one of the former firefighters, as a storyteller for the site. During World War II, Bishop had been too young to go to war, but on the homefront, women and young men served in "man-sized" jobs and collected "man-sized" paychecks. It was a rude awakening when the soldiers came home, and Bishop had a hard time finding the employment he'd grown accustomed to. In 1947 when he heard about "the dorm deal at the old county jail" they were offering for fire fighters, Bishop signed up. He was able to tell his audience the changes that had been made in the building and what life had been like then. While showing where the men lined up their bunks, he said nobody thought anything of placing their bunk over the hanging trapdoor. Plaques line some of the walls, and at least one had Bishop's name on it. He said, "It was for suffering twenty-five years as a fireman."

Once a new fire station and city hall were built in the mid-1960s, the old jail stood vacant and deteriorating, largely from the rising damp that was weakening the walls. Fortunately, some far-sighted citizens took it over to house the Hidalgo County Historical Museum.

Bars once removed from the windows have been reconstructed, and though repairs were made throughout, upkeep is an on-going process. A welcome addition that the prisoners and jailer's family never enjoyed is the installation of air-conditioning when the museum opened to the public in 1970. So popular was the museum that a new wing was added by 1977. Then in 2003, a $5.5 million expansion made it truly a state-of-the-art facility, and the name has been expanded as well to represent far more than merely one county. It is now the Museum of South Texas History.

By the 1980s, Edinburg's placement on the rail line and also on the intersection of two major highways made it the "gateway city" to the fertile Rio Grande Valley, and tourism has become big business. Many "winter Texans" escape the cold of their northern home states each year, and the museum gives young and old plenty to see. The museum sponsors educational programs using guided and self-guided tours. It has museum classes, hands-on activities for children, lectures, demonstrations, interpretive drama, and offers a school/museum cooperative curriculum.

Museum personnel report that of all the wonderful exhibits they have, the old jail with a hanging room is still one of the most popular attractions. Exhibits in the old jail include photographs and such artifacts as a ball and chain and an unusual kind of leg iron called an "ankle spur," in which rods are attached at the side, that at best would make walking difficult, and at worst impossible.

Look for the Old Jail on the historic county square, a white two-story building with a red roof. For information about visiting times or tours, contact: Museum of South Texas History, 121 E. McIntyre, Edinburg, TX 78541. (956) 383-6911 or visit their website at: www.mosthistory.org

*Hidalgo County Jail current appearance.*

# Edna
# Jackson County Jail
## (1922-1981)
### Texana Museum and Otto &
### Virginia Lawrence Children's Museum
### and Part of the La Salle Odyssey

E dna's 1922 jail, which houses the Otto & Virginia Lawrence Children's Museum, stands back to back with the Texana Museum-library, and both are operated by the Texana Museum and Library Association. Sound like a double treat? Make that triple, because the Association takes part in the Texas Historical Commission project the "La Salle Odyssey," which includes seven museums and six counties along and near the Texas coast to give an understanding of France's ill-fated expedition in 1686. Edna's exhibit covers the Karankawa tribe's role in the La Salle saga. More about this "French connection" later—first let's visit the old jail.

Judge Harrison Stafford told me this jail continued in service through 1981 without heating, and certainly without air-conditioning. While a sheriff's family lived in the first floor apartment, prisoners could get at least some heat when the sheriff opened the kitchen door to the upstairs cells, but no jailer lived there after 1954. When the last family moved out of the sheriff's quarters, additional jail space was made available on the first floor. At closing time, the whole jail would be locked down with no phone or other contact with the outside. Judge Stafford remembers seeing long strings running from light bulbs in the corridor into the cells by which the prisoners could turn on the lights. Originally there were two community cells that held about four prisoners each. Two separate cells were intended for women or the insane, and there was one isolation cell for a dangerous prisoner.

Lewis Watson, Jr., the son of two sheriffs—yes, two—grew up in the jail from third grade through high school. This was the last family that lived in the jail. His father served as county sheriff from 1941-1969, and when he died in office, Lewis Jr.'s mother, Frankie, finished the last year of her husband's term as sheriff. While they lived in the jail, Mrs. Watson cooked two meals a day for the prisoners, and a trustee prepared a simpler third meal upstairs.

Memories for Lewis Jr. were mostly good. His friends always found visits to the jail fun, and when there weren't many prisoners, his dad would give the boys a thrill by locking them up temporarily. Lewis Jr. found it exciting when his dad brought in a new prisoner into the separate jail part. The boy would pull up a chair to the window of the house door that connected with the jail. There he would crack the window, listen, and learn some new vocabulary.

Lewis Jr. said his bedroom was directly beneath the cell for the mentally ill, where the metal bunks were suspended on chains. Many a night, a prisoner would raise, then slam down his or her bunk, jolting Lewis awake. He begged his father to move those prisoners to a cell over the living room where such nocturnal noises wouldn't bother anyone, but because of the configuration of cells, it couldn't be done. He also remembers a more pleasant sound though. When the congregation in the church across the street sang hymns, the prisoners would often join in.

In those days, trustees were allowed to work in the fields during planting and harvesting time, thus earning money to pay off fines they owed. Lewis pointed out that no one ever tried out the gallows, but it's still in place in the old jail as a trapdoor and a ring in the ceiling above.

When a new jail replaced this one in 1981, the Texana Museum and Library Association stepped in and found a totally different purpose for the building. Otto and Virginia Lawrence, key members in the association, came up with the idea to use the old jail as a museum for children, so the group named it in their honor. Museum Curator Mary Sales says the pint-size visitors get a kick out of the turn-of-the-century country store, post office, and classroom. There's a claw foot bathtub with pillows for a kid or two to curl up and read. Vintage clothes are available to play dress-up, and homemade games are a curiosity to modern kids.

Youngsters and grownups alike want to look at the cells upstairs. The younger set may just want to stay where they can play when adults and older kids go next door to the Texana Museum. Some of the antiques there are well over a hundred years old and represent the life of the early Texas settlers.

This is also where the La Salle Odyssey displays its exhibit on Native Americans. In 1686 when La Salle came ashore, instead of meeting the friendly tribes in the area, his expedition had the misfortune of encountering the fierce, cannibalistic Karankawas, who had no intention of sharing their land with invaders. La Salle had been stacking up an unbelievable number of misfortunes even before that. The worst of these was his mistaken belief that he had landed at the mouth of the Mississippi River, which he had claimed as "Louisiana" on an earlier expedition, in the name of France's King Louis XIV. About 400 miles off course, he was in fact at Matagorda Bay, where he sank his ship *La Belle* (in recent years found and excavated). The Edna exhibit shows how the Karankawas lived and how they were instrumental in the demise of the expedition. Meanwhile La Salle, leading a troop on foot to search for the Mississippi, eventually was murdered by his own men.

Whether or not you decide to also visit other museums in the Odyssey series, you have to admire the Texas Historical Commission's concept of tying them together as segments of an important era in Texas History at the locations where the events took place. Had La Salle accomplished his goals, we might be talking to each other and museum docents in French. And we'd be touring a *bastille* instead of the old Texas jail that can be found at the corner of Cypress and Ed Linn Streets.

For information about visiting times or tours, contact: Texana Museum, 403 N. Wells, Edna, TX 77957. (361) 782-5431 or visit their website at: www.ykc.com/jccc/historic_interest.htm To print a brochure of the entire Odyssey, go to: www.thc.state.tx.us/lasalle/pdfs/Odyssey.pdf

*Jackson County Jail current appearance.*
*Courtesy of Texana Museum Association.*

*Courtesy of* Jackson County Herald-Tribune
*editor/photographer Chris Lundstrom.*

# Fairfield
# Freestone County Jail
## (1879-1913)
### Freestone County Museum

An air of mystery prevails at the old Fairfield Jail. When I first began investigation on the internet, I encountered confusion about which jail has been made into the museum. I began to see why, considering that three of them were built between the years of 1852 and 1913.

It turns out that the museum is housed in the third jail, which was built in 1879. Curator Molly Fryer believes much of the confusion comes from the fact that the foundation of the 1857 Jail #2 is on the same grounds. However, official drawings and photos confirm a definite difference.

Next came the controversy of whether or not this jail had a gallows, and if so, whether it was ever used. After being in service as "the" Freestone County Jail for a mere thirty-three years, it was converted into a home when yet another jail replaced it. No hanging device was apparent to residents, but then, such an appliance would hardly have been a selling point for home-makers. Of course, bars on the windows, and the two cells upstairs were removed. This unusually thick-walled structure housed a single family for a while. Then the interior was reconfigured to create separate apartments, usually two families, but at one time four families. The stairway was moved from the east wall, where the line is still visible, to the center of the build-ing where a newer wall separates the apartments.

Residents and their visitors through the years have talked about a "hole" under the ground-level floor. The son of owner Tommy Willard told that when working on the floor for his dad and having to crawl around under-

79

neath, he found a hole. A lady visiting the museum recounted that, when she was around three years old, she and her brothers and sisters used to play in the hole. The game was "hanging"—and as the youngest, she always had to play the victim. If children could climb out of the opening, it couldn't have been very deep. Several former residents have reported the presence of the hole, and some were unaccountably frightened of it.

I had heard of a "hanging hole" in one other jail before. Typically, any jail's gallows are placed in the highest position available. In this case, dropping the prisoner from an opening in the second floor to the lower floor was probably not sufficient to break his neck. A hole may have been provided on the first floor to make up the rest of the distance. At the Fairfield Jail, Molly Fryer suspects the stairway was moved to a spot to utilize the second floor gallows opening for the stairwell. Is it merely coincidence that the landing now at the top of the stairs is even with that mysterious hole in the ground? The sister of former owner Tommy Willard, Mrs. Doris Goodman, lived on the west side apartment in the late fifties. Mr. James, living on the east side, told her that in his part of the house there was a hinged cover, which had been used for a person hanged to drop below ground. He said this hinged cover was behind and under the staircase. The hole today is filled and covered with a metal plate.

Roy Hill is a lawyer living in Fairfield. His sheriff great grandfather and his grandfather, Deputy Roy Burleson, served in office together. Deputy Burleson delivered the last meal to prisoners in this jail before moving them to the new structure on the courthouse square in 1913. Hill remembers his grandfather talking about a hanging gallows in the jail.

While all the above may be only hearsay, the clues do stack up to solve the mystery, and records of hangings further confirm it. Documents state that the county's fourth legal hanging took place "within the walls of the county jail," and the date of that hanging was during the time when the 1879 jail was in use. With that, I rest my case about the hanging hole.

Which bad guys spent time here in the 1879 jail? The "baddest," John Wesley Hardin, spent a night in this jail while on his way back to the town of Comanche to face trial for murder. The next morning, the two officers in charge were taking Hardin out of town when they realized they had left their lunch at the saloon. While the deputy went back to get it, Hardin caught the sheriff off guard, killed him with his own gun, and escaped.

The jail also housed good guys. Nat Davis Riley gave the museum a note from the early 1900s when his father, J.P. Riley had been the jailer. A trusted prisoner had written the note to Riley, warning him of an escape plot. Two dangerous prisoners planned to attack him and steal his keys when he brought breakfast the next morning. This warning not only foiled the jailbreak, but may have also saved Riley's life.

That note is but one of hundreds of artifacts and papers donated by citizens to the museum. These objects range from the priceless to the bizarre, such as a prosthetic leg from an unknown user. The museum is frozen in the era when the building was turned from a jail into a home. The bottom floor was not greatly different except for the moving of the stairs. The upper floor, made homey and attractive, has almost no reminders of having been the jail, but the prisoner's bathtub is still there. The one of a kind oversized tub is on wheels so it could be pulled by its wagon tongue from cell to cell, and all prisoners would take their turn bathing in the same water.

The museum extends outside to historic buildings and objects that have been moved in. Prominent at the front of the building is a bell that, believe it or not, was recovered from a sunken riverboat in the Trinity River not far away. Displays in the log cabin especially convey an understanding of the pioneer lifestyle. On the other hand, a generously-sized outhouse, fitted with modern plumbing, shows that the management understands to just what extent visitors are willing to experience the past.

One more mystery—one day a couple were touring the museum, and when they came downstairs, the man asked, "Where is the other set of stairs?" Jo, the volunteer, told him there was only one, but the man insisted, "As I was going upstairs I saw a woman walk across from the parlor to the other room, but when I went in, there was no one there. She has to have gone down another way."

The curator and a few volunteers say the atmosphere at the museum is okay during the day, except for a few unexplained noises and cold drafts. At night the feeling of being watched is "too much." Fryer also says that on more than one occasion, she has found the barred front door standing open in the morning when she knows she locked it the previous night. Fortunately, visiting hours are in the daytime.

The old jail is a block east of the courthouse. For information about visiting times or tours, contact: Freestone County Museum, 302 E. Main, Fairfield, TX 75840. (903) 389-3738, e-mail the museum at fcmuseum@airport.net or visit their website at: www.fairfieldtx.com

*Freestone County Jail current appearance.*

*Other historic buildings on the grounds help make up the museum complex.*

*Wilson County Jail circa January 1926; "Biggest snowfall in thirty-one years."*
*Courtesy of the Wilson County Historical Society.*

## Floresville
# Wilson County Jail
## (1887-1974)
### Wilson County Jailhouse Museum

Southwest Texas always surprises me with its blend of grace and harsh reality. The larger than usual number of Texas Rangers mentioned in area history indicates a violent past. But then there's that more gracious side too.

The San Antonio River runs alongside what is now the town of Floresville, extending San Antonio's Spanish mission influence of the latter 1600s. Spain used missions, the way early Americans used forts, to gain a foothold on the land. The Spanish then peopled the area by converting as many Native tribes to Christianity as they could and importing settlers from as far away as the

Canary Islands. The name "Flores" entered the scene when a Spanish land grant was awarded to that family, who built ranches along the river.

An heiress of part of that land was Josefa Augustina Flores, a descendent of Texas Revolutionary War veterans, Jose Flores and Juan Seguin. By 1871, a new county seat was slated for Wilson County (named after James Charles Wilson, Texas patriot and Methodist minister). Josefa Flores donated 200 acres for a town to be built in honor of her ancestor, Francisco Flores de Abrego. Citizens named this new county seat Floresville, and Josefa's husband, Samuel Barker, became the first county sheriff.

The first courthouse, a simple structure, burned down after only ten years. The magnificent courthouse now standing was built at a new site in 1883. Four years later, on the same square, a new jail replaced the old one, which was too far away and no longer adequate. Both the courthouse and the jail on the town's square demonstrate the grace that citizens had come to expect.

The usual living quarters for the sheriff's family was provided. With no bars on the front windows, even on the upstairs windows, at first sight I wouldn't have known it was a jail, had it not been for the sign. I soon learned the design for this jail is different. The family apartment occupies the first floor with a front entryway but also has two bedrooms upstairs. The jail could accommodate thirty-two prisoners, and was of course separated from the home. A steel door opened from the dining room into the jail area so that food could be taken to the cells. A steel back door admitted and released prisoners, and all the windows in the jail section are fitted with metal bars. Metal stairs in this area lead to three levels of cell blocks with runabouts, the top level being for solitary confinement.

Another set of stairs leads to a trapdoor above a long drop for the gallows. One hanging was attempted here, but the device malfunctioned. As one person put it, "The prisoner almost died." How the matter ended is not recorded.

Texas Ranger Captain W.L. "Will" Wright got his start in law enforcement as a Wilson County sheriff's deputy when he was twenty-four in 1892. As a Ranger, he was credited with the saying, "Mean as hell—had to kill him." Apparently, he himself furnished the meanness required for the law of the times. While Captain Wright's duty was patrolling the Mexican border for smugglers, he earned the epithet, "el capitan diablo" (the devil captain). But he was also fair as the following story shows.

In 1897, a ranch hand named Maximo Martinez became dissatisfied with his job, his wife, and his children. He tried to persuade a girl named

Juanita to run away with him, but she declined. Maximo went to her house with an ax and brutally murdered Juanita and her grandparents. Friends of the family went after him as vigilantes. Texas Ranger Will Wright formed a posse and trailed him for five days before catching up with him. Outwitting the lynch mob, Wright took Maximo to the Wilson County Jail. In a trial Maximo was convicted and legally sentenced to hang by the neck until dead.

Because the indoor hanging device had proved unreliable before, a scaffold was constructed just outside the jail. A mob of thousands showed up. Maximo appeared on the platform in a suit with artificial orange blossoms pinned to his lapel. He sang a song about his "fickle" Juanita, smoked a cigar, and warned others not to follow in his footsteps. Reporter, Sam Woolford (*San Antonio Light*, article printed 1957), made the rather large claim that Maximo's hanging "was the most spectacular and picturesque event of its kind that ever took place in the state."

In the 1940s, a latter day prisoner named Joe spent enough time in the Wilson County slammer to write his memoirs—in neat, one-and-a-half-inch block lettering. You have to wonder how a prisoner came by tools that could etch the steel so deeply that aluminum paint can't hide his words. What's more, they appear on all four walls. Ralph Gerhardt, of the Wilson County Historical Society, has put together a booklet of the writings and also looked up Joe's jail records. It seems his crimes ran from "affrays" (fights) to burglary. Quotes are verbatim, and we can excuse a few errors considering there would be no way to correct such painstaking carvings. One line of thought says, "Have robber and stold all my life but . . . I love all [?] women and lot of money and a good car to take my baby out in." His crimes must have escalated judging by this message, "Will you write to me Huntsville Texas, Box 32," perhaps his last.

The old jail served until 1974 when a more modern facility was built. Fortunately, the Wilson County Historical Society turned the 1887 Jail into a museum.

The softer side of this building is of course the part that was a home, and walking through the beautifully furnished rooms gives the visitor a feeling of what life was like in the old days. Historical Society member Louise Thurman says all the items have been donated, which makes it truly Wilson County's Museum. One item of interest is a fireproof safe from the first courthouse. Some had begrudged the expense when it was purchased, but it proved worth the investment by saving the records when the courthouse burned down.

Events such as a "haunted house" at Halloween may draw visitors in, but the charm of the home and the starkness of the jail make them want to come back for a closer look at the furnishings and printed material. You'll find the Jailhouse Museum on the courthouse square.

For information about visiting times or tours, contact: Wilson County Historical Society, 1142 C Street, P.O. Box 101, Floresville, TX 78114. (830) 216-2225 or (830) 393-2792 or visit their website at: www.wilsoncountyhistory.com/Jailhouse_Museum.htm

*Wilson County Jail current appearance.*

*Fort Stockton Military Guardhouse.*

# Fort Stockton
# Two Jails
## Military Guardhouse (1867-1886)

The pre-Civil War Camp Stockton occupied a strategic site where several trails connected at Comanche Springs, a location where approximately 65,000,000 gallons of water flowed through per day. These routes also happened to cross the Comanche war trail.

Secretary of War Jefferson Davis made this fort one of the bases for his pet project, the U.S. Camel Corps, an experiment for the arid, rugged Big Bend country. Although the project was working, Washington dropped the concept when Texas seceded from the Union, and Jeff Davis became President of the Confederate States of America. Federal troops abandoned the camp and the seventy-seven camels to the Confederates, who subsequently abandoned the site as well. Some of the camels were sold, others released into the desert where Indians and frontiersmen had little problem hunting the domesticated beasts to extinction. Head camel driver Hadji Ali, who the soldiers called "Hi Jolly," took a few to Arizona for his freight hauling business, but after the business failed, he too released his camels. Some claim that their ghosts still roam the desert. At any rate, both the camels and any vestige of Camp Stockton were gone by the end of the war in 1865.

The westward movement surged forward as wave after wave of U.S. citizens followed the lure of cheap or free land, adventure, gold strikes, or the chance to escape tainted pasts. Not surprisingly, Indians took issue with those who competed for water, slaughtered the buffalo herds, their main sustenance, and invaded land that had been theirs. Because of this, the settlers demanded protection from the "savages."

The U.S. government answered by building or rebuilding a string of forts along the western frontier. One of these was Fort Stockton, moved a short distance from the original camp site. Politicians solved two problems by combining the need for more soldiers with the need to provide jobs for newly freed slaves. Blacks had fought in American wars since the French and Indian War and the American Revolution, but not until the Civil War had as many as 180,000 proven themselves in battle. In 1866, Congress enacted the precedent of creating entire regiments of inexperienced black enlisted men under the command of trained white officers.

Cavalrymen were first sent to protect settlers flooding across the West. Later came infantrymen, whom the Native Americans called "walk-a-heaps." They also assigned a better known name to the blacks, "buffalo soldiers." According to tradition, this was because the troopers' curly hair reminded them of a buffalo's mane, but the identity with buffalo had deeper roots too. During the years of Indian hostility, buffalo soldiers gained a reputation for toughness, bravery, and dedication. Recognizing that the Indians would not have named anyone after an animal they revered unless they also transferred respect, the Tenth Cavalry added the image of a buffalo to their regimental crest. Not until 1907 was the Indian Wars Campaign Medal created and some awarded to those early buffalo soldiers.

In 1873, a near mutiny at the fort occurred, calling for a general court martial and subsequent need for a guardhouse. Capt. Francis C. Dodge, the commander of the fort, had received a complaint against the post surgeon, Peter Cleary, signed by a majority of the enlisted men. It charged that Dr. Cleary refused to treat Pvt. John Taylor when he claimed to be ill. The doctor refused to excuse him from duty. Other men in the company covered for him, until Taylor again sought treatment. Dr. Cleary ordered that, for malingering, he should be locked in the guardhouse overnight and then sent to work the next day. Taylor became so ill on the job he had to be carried to the hospital, where he later died. When even an autopsy didn't reveal a cause of death, Dr. Cleary said the man believed he was "hoodooed" and worried himself to death.

At that point, sixty-two of the fort's enlisted men, who believed the doctor had poisoned Taylor, rose up, threatening the officers' lives. The insubordinate men were arrested, several of the non-commissioned officers were locked in the guardhouse, and a court-martial was held, presided over by Maj. Z.R. Bliss from Fort Davis. Those convicted got five to fifteen years in the penitentiary.

By 1886, the Indian Wars were over, and the fort closed down. It sat neglected until historians secured a grant and began restoration in 1981. Only four buildings remained intact, one of which is the guardhouse. Constructed of cut stone with timbers that had to be hauled by oxcart all the way from Indianola on the coast, this building is as stark looking today as it must have been when prisoners were held there. The front room, where officers admitted "guests," is strictly no-frills, though it has a fireplace. It displays a few exhibits and explains the type of punishment administered. The back room has shackles attached to the walls by iron rings. Even a windowless solitary confinement room, in the middle of the building, has thick stone walls.

Rumor has it that the guardhouse is haunted. One of the staff members asked if I had felt anything odd in there. I had to confess to a feeling of discomfort in the back room, something I can only describe as an unexplainable sadness. "That's it," the staff member concurred.

Other buildings, such as the barracks show comprehensive exhibits and more are being developed all the time. Also check with the office and gift shop for details about an annual event in March, "Texas History Days," that includes costumed reenactments.

*Pecos County Jail circa 1883. Courtesy of the Fort Stockton Historical Society.*

# The Pecos County Jail
# (1883-1975)

From the time the fort became active again, the town of Fort Stockton grew up around it, so much a part of the fort as to use the same name. Civilian lawbreakers were housed in the military guardhouse until the Pecos County jail was built in 1883. Up to 1882, a privately owned house had served as the courthouse, but that year the county passed a bond to build both a courthouse and a jail.

You couldn't ask for a more hospitable appearance than this jail—unless you were about to be locked behind its bars. The first floor provided quarters for the sheriff. Hangings were conducted down the street on a certain tree until a scaffold device was built in the third story of the jail. Once hanging as the state's method of execution ended, the section was completely sealed off. Past president of the Historical Commission, Lee Harris, assured me it's still there.

The first and second floors were remodeled and enlarged in 1913, and steel cages were installed on the second floor. Sheriff Doug Barker's family lived there at the time. Only Sheriff Clarence (Pete) Ten Eyck served longer than Barker. A new jail replaced this one in 1975, and the city turned the old jail over to the Pecos County Historical Commission. The Commission allowed a sheriff or a deputy's family to continue living on the first floor until 2000. Pretty enough to be a B&B, this building is again undergoing renovation, this time to be a law enforcement museum.

Both facilities are owned by the city and managed by the Pecos County Historical Commission. Historical Fort Stockton is at 301 E. Third St. (2 blocks east of Main Street; follow signs). For information about visiting times or tours, contact: (432) 336-2400. The county jail is on the corner across the street from the courthouse on Main Street. For information about visiting times or tours, contact: Historical Commission Chair: (432) 336-3151. For both facilities, you may also ask information from the curator at the Annie Riggs Memorial Museum across the street from the courthouse, or the Chamber of Commerce, P.O. Box 1000, Fort Stockton, TX 79735. 1-800-336-2166 or (432) 336-8052 or visit their website at: www.ci.fort-stockton.tx.us

*Today's enlarged Pecos County Jail.*

# Gatesville
# Coryell County Jail
## (1855-1875)
## Coryell County Museum Exhibit

For all the moving around Gatesville's old log jail has done through the years, it should have been built on wheels. But in 1855 the newly-founded town's first priority was any kind of hoosegow they could build. In the words of R.L. (Uncle Bob) Saunders, "They weren't no money for a court house, but the public demanded that a jail be built. When John Turney, our first high sheriff, chained his prisoners, hoss thieves though they were, to the oak trees that were scattered around on the square, right out in the open for the wolves and vermin to chaw on, that brought on talk" (excerpted from *Down Memory Lane*, A Compilation of Saunder's columns, written 1946-1951, for the *Gatesville Messenger & Star-Forum*, published by the Coryell County Museum and Historical Center).

John H. Chrisman contracted to build a double-log structure with an underground dungeon at a cost of $1,400. I knew the historical hoosegow had been moved under the Coryell County Museum's roof, but I was unprepared for what I encountered before reaching the object of my quest.

First, the big museum sign and window display looked like that of an upscale retail store. Once a mini-mall, the building greeted visitors with a large entry hall surrounded by "store" space. Balconies overlook the first floor. To the right is the Museum's gift shop, but everything else is filled with museum exhibits, artistically displayed, and more rooms extend beyond these as well. I all but forgot the jail I'd come to see.

A staff member stated that when the building was acquired, the organization brought in a museum consultant for planning—and then board members and volunteers went to work. Prison labor from the new jail was used, and even at present, county jail prisoners do the cleaning. All of this results in a highly professional appearance. Types of artifacts are too numerous to name here, but the most valuable is a 6,000-piece spur collection, with properties dating from the Crusades. Showmanship is everything in the way artifacts are grouped into scenes or displayed as if in stores. Upstairs or by way of an attractive, open elevator, is what had been a restaurant. There you'll find more, including a special area for children's events.

Revenue comes in from the gift shop and a once-private club in the complex, which is now rented out for weddings, parties, and dances—but the museum has not always been so well off. In 1947, when local leaders first intended to build a more modest museum, they asked everyone in the county to donate a dollar, but the effort failed. Nevertheless, board members kept collecting artifacts of all kinds and storing them wherever space could be found, so that when a building was obtained, there would be plenty of things to fill it.

The group's prime goal was to purchase and save Gatesville's first public building, the log jail, but it was a long wait before that goal came to fruition. The old jail had stayed in constant service for about twenty years, and according to Mildred Watkins Mears in her Texas Sesquicentennial book, *Coryell County Scrapbook*, prisoners were in it at all times. Guards were hired as needed at one to three dollars a day depending on how dangerous the prisoners were. Various individuals and eating establishments contracted for food service. Mears wrote that during W.W. Hammack's tenure as sheriff, "a man was taken from the jail and hanged by a mob, and there may have been others. Another escaped and the county offered $250 for his capture." Uncle Bob Saunders, in one of his columns, called this practice, "ole Judge Lynch [getting] the boys together for a little Hanging Bee."

In 1876 the jail was moved out of town. The historical marker states that the building was used as a smokehouse, but local legend says it was part of the County Poor Farm. At last, in 1980 the jail was moved back into Gatesville to Raby Park on Museum grounds. Historians even recreated an underground dungeon like the original. A trapdoor, less than a yard square, just inside the door, closed off the opening. With headroom only four feet high, "good" prisoners were allowed above ground inside the cabin with the guard or sheriff. "Bad" prisoners stayed below except for occasional relief when they got to go outside and be chained to a tree.

By 1998, the Museum had a space for the old hoosegow, in a huge warehouse adjoining the back of the facility through an oversized garage door. Every log was numbered, dismantled, and the old structure was rebuilt inside. I found it much larger than I had expected, but the exposed ends of the logs at the corners reveal the ingenuity of the double-log construction. Inside you may first mistake a couple of very small barred openings for windows, but they're purely for ventilation. Matching "windows" outside are off-set several feet away so that no one could chip his way through. Needless to say, the interior allows little light. And the dungeon? It must have been as dark as a cave. The concrete floor of the warehouse makes replication unfeasible, but the trapdoor remains in place to give visitors the idea. Old-timers reported the sheriff placing his rocking chair over the trapdoor and rocking back and forth to remind those below of his presence.

The space is appropriately shared by such exhibits as wagons and a giant-sized iron door salvaged from the second jail, which didn't last nearly so long as this "temporary" one. Yes, the old girl has at last found a permanent home, and she won't be needing those wheels after all. Best of all, she looks sturdy enough to thwart the most determined escape artist if she were ever called into service again.

For information about visiting times or tours, contact: Coryell County Museum, 718 Main St., P.O. Box 24, Gatesville, TX 76528. (254) 865-5007 or visit their website at: www.coryellmuseum.org

*The 1855 log jail moved indoors.*

*Gigantic door from the second jail, the last relic of the "improved jail."*

*(l to r) Deputy N.D. Cone, County Clerk Charles Ramsey, Jailer Boone Jackson, Sheriff W.W. (Bill) Johnston circa 1902-1914. Courtesy of Gonzales County Record Center and Archives.*

# Gonzales
# Gonzales County Jail Museum
## (1887-1975)

### Chamber of Commerce and County Jail Museum

We shouldn't be surprised that the "Come-and-Take-It" town of Gonzales is peopled with a feisty and spirited lot. Everyone in town seems to know stories about the old county jail as well as a docent might. One look at the jail and the adjacent courthouse shows that, small town or not, these people are in the habit of taking care of things for themselves. The jail is a veritible prison equipped to hold 150 to 200 prisoners "in case of a riot."

Over the years, the county conducted six legal hangings. The outdoor 1878 hanging of Brown Bowen attracted a crowd of about 4,000 observers, so when the gallows were built inside the 1887 jail, a large viewing area was planned to accommodate a crowd. Ironically it was only used twice. Another bit of irony is that, wherever Bowen is buried, his tombstone isn't with him but instead is on display at the museum. Bowen swore to the end that it was his brother-in-law, John Wesley Hardin, who committed the murder in question. But no one believed him.

Even though the Hardins' christened their son after the famous preacher John Wesley, the namesake did not make him kindhearted. You may hear that the notorious gunslinger was locked in this jail, but he wasn't—only because the state prison got him first. Hardin spent his time at the state pen reading the law. When he got out, Hardin hung up his lawyer shingle right there in Gonzales, where he lived until he was gunned down in El Paso.

The last legal hanging done in Gonzales provided the town with one of its most lasting legends. My husband Don was setting up his camera tripod when Leon Netardus, author of *Ghosts of Gonzales*, happened along and introduced himself. He told us why the four faces of the clock on the courthouse next-door won't keep the right time. Albert Howard, convicted of a brutal murder, was sentenced to hang. He swore his innocence till the bitter end, and "proved" it by issuing a curse on the clock tower. He told everyone those clocks would never keep the same time again, and they haven't. In fact, lightning has struck the tower a couple of times to boot. A great deal of money has been spent on clock repair over the years, but it never lasts.

At least Howard was granted his final request, to be baptized. A preacher came in and performed the ceremony in a bathtub in the sheriff's quarters, and that bathtub is presently on museum display.

Another legend made its way into a movie, *The Ballad of Gregorio Cortez,* with the Gonzales Jail, the Courthouse, and many Gonzaleans included in the filming. Gregorio Cortez had allegedly stolen horses in Karnes County and was headed toward Gonzales. In 1901, Sheriff Richard Glover took a posse and went after him. In a shoot-out, Cortez killed the sheriff and a deputy. After quite a chase, the Texas Rangers captured him and locked him up in the Gonzales Jail. A mob gathered to lynch him, but newly appointed Sheriff Frank Fly (later Judge Fly) talked them out of it and took Cortez to the San Antonio Jail where emotions were less volatile. Although he pleaded self-defense, the court found him guilty. Cortez received a lengthy sentence but managed to get paroled. To this day, the saga is controversial.

A later series of frequent liquor store burglaries had local law enforcement officers perplexed. The thieves would steal only a bottle or two of booze and a few packages of cigarettes at a time. Sheriff L.O. McGinty knew the two usual suspects were already in jail, so he sent a deputy to check out the third floor where the suspects were currently residing. These prisoners had been climbing up to the top of the cells, escaping through the attic that led to the flat roof, and then climbing down the drain pipe. After replenishing their supply of smokes and drinks, they would return the same way and be found sleeping peacefully in their bunks when breakfast was served in the morning. Their method of operation came to an abrupt end when that section of cells was sealed off.

While McGinty held office from 1951 to 1969, his daughter, Sandra Wolff, grew up in the jail. She told me that although she never tried the prisoners' escape route, she did look to see how they did it. Her mom was such a good cook, one of the jail's regular "customers" used to time his drunk-and-disorderly escapades to get arrested in time for supper. As for her dad, at six feet tall, and 210 pounds, his friends said his initials stood for "Little Orvon." She recalls deputies and Judge Fly as her best friends. Any time she would climb through the window into the judge's office, he would close up and take her for a walk around the square for a cherry Coke and cookies. But when she was a teenager, any boy who dated her had to be brave. With two or three lawmen standing by to see that she got in safely, there was no such thing as a goodnight kiss. Sandra is now the manager of Pioneer Village, just out of Gonzales.

These days the Chamber of Commerce occupies the space that had been the sheriff's home. Visitors enter a large room that used to be the sheriff's office where they can pick up a self-guided tour brochure. Here and in surrounding areas are numerous exhibits, all of which either belonged to Gonzales County law officers or were confiscated from prisoners. An assortment of weapons taken away from criminals includes a homemade ring knife made from a spoon. One that saddened me was a child's baseball bat. The six-year-old who owned it had been beaten to death with it by his mother.

Exhibits run from the earliest days to the more recent, such as a two-way radio. Before that invention, the Gonzales sheriff turned on a red light atop the jail to alert deputies to come in. A list of infractions that could lead to arrest is still posted on the wall. One of these infractions was, "general principles."

Off the entry hall are three particularly interesting rooms. The first, the deputy's or jailer's bedroom, is furnished as in the old days, looking peaceful and homey. At the very end of the hall is the dungeon, a dark metal walled room, for which the only light and air that came into the room were through a few small holes above the iron door. You are cautioned not to enter this "as it is dangerous," and I was not tempted—on general principles.

Between the appealing and the abominable is the appalling—a "women's and lunatics' cell." When a woman was arrested, it wasn't uncommon to lock up her children with her. For example, while Gregorio Cortez was eluding the law, members of his family were arrested, most likely on the charge of harboring a fugitive, but also to lure Cortez to give himself up. This would have been the room where they stayed.

Cell blocks on the second and third floors still stand, complete with interesting graffiti. For several years before the jail closed in 1975, only the two-story high runaround was used for prisoners since the cell blocks had proven insecure. Visible to second and third floor cells, especially the three death cells, the gallows served as something to contemplate to the inhabitants. The structure was removed in the 1950s, and the present is a replica.

With the Chamber of Commerce housed in this magnificent old building, visitors are welcome everyday except major holidays. Contact: Chamber of Commerce & Gonzales County Jail Museum, 414 St. Lawrence Street, Gonzales, TX. 830-672-6532 or visit their website at: www.gonzalestexas.com/visitor/attractions.asp

*Gonzales County Jail current appearance.*

*Hood County Jail circa 1886. Photo courtesy of the Hood County Jail Museum.*

# Granbury
# Hood County Jail
## (1886-1978)
### Old Jail Museum

Granbury's knack for playing on its history as a tourist attraction is something of a phenomenon. Just about any day of the week, you'll see visitors strolling the square, and during events, it may be downright crowded. But busy as they are, merchants and friendly citizens are quick to say, "Have you been to see such-and-such?" The Old Jail Museum is frequently mentioned.

The jail, built in 1886, replaced a thirteen-year-old log jail. The building's classified as late Victorian style, exemplified beautifully in the first floor sheriff's quarters. But the foreboding, fortress-like exterior, complete with hanging tower, must have made many a prisoner's heart skip a beat at seeing it for the first time. The stone walls are almost two feet thick, and if you look closely outside, you may see Roman numerals carved into some of the blocks. These were the notations assigned to local stone masons to record payment due for a certain number of blocks they placed.

The smaller building in the back was an afterthought. With the main building almost completed, somebody realized there was no kitchen! For $500 more, and using leftover stone, the builders added the small, separate house with a dog trot (not enclosed until about 1909).

The main cell block includes riveted strap-iron cages with floor and ceiling made of solid metal for the most dangerous prisoners. Others could move around in a larger area. The whole room could be locked down by a steel door. Its hanging tower was never used, although at least one hanging took place before the jail was built.

What was life like for a resident jailer and his family? Charles Locklin of Austin, grandson to Marshal Charles Edward Locklin (tenure 1906-1917), has been researching to find out. Looking in court records for the various situations his grandfather handled, he discovered a few infractions were: "speeding" (on horses), "cursing over the telephone" (must have been listeners on the party line), "refusing to work on the roads" (all property owners were supposed to contribute time for these improvements), and "leaving his horse not securely tied to a chair on the sidewalk" (guess you had to be there to understand this one).

Mr. Locklin also shared the interviews he had recorded of his aunt, the marshal's daughter, Ora Locklin Ellis. She and her three siblings had spent some growing-up time in the living quarters during their father's tenure. Ora tells of a woman prisoner, put in the "insane room," who broke a window with her hand, bit a chunk out of her own sliced hand, and then wiped blood all over the walls. The prisoner then told Marshal Locklin, "I'm washing you all to Hell." It took both the marshal and the sheriff to subdue her by throwing a sheet over her. A doctor treated her hand and "fixed her arm so she couldn't get her hand to her mouth." She was eventually sent to the state hospital.

One horse thief spent quite some time in the jail waiting for his trial because the court was only held twice a year. Ora, about sixteen at the time, was starting out for school one morning when the prisoner called to her, asking if she would come up and get a letter he wanted her to mail. When she did, she found the letter was addressed to her. The rustler asked if she would marry him after he got out of trouble. She never went around him again.

A later officer, Constable J.B. Hall (tenure 1954-1957), also housed his family at the Hood County Jail, and two of his children related their experiences. Hall's son Ron said he hadn't been home much in those days because he was in high school at the time and already working at radio broadcasting, a profession he followed as an adult. He does remember sitting in his 1950 Dodge, parked next to the jail, with his buddies with whom he had a band. They were all fans of "Louisiana Hayride," and all that steel in the building made for perfect radio reception.

By that day and age, dangerous prisoners were transported to higher security jails, probably in nearby Fort Worth. The prisoners held in the Hood County Jail weren't violent, and many were only weekend drunks. Ron says they were more likely to have break-ins than break-outs. Not only was the cell block left open, many of the cells were, too. Once he came home to find a prisoner raiding the family refrigerator for a snack.

Ron's sister, Sandra Hall Hayes, was age nine to eleven while the family lived there, so she had a lot more experiences to remember. A couple of the inmates were regulars, and she remembers a time when one of them was telling her mother how much he appreciated the meals she served. "I'll try to come back next weekend," he said. He did, but with a broken hand from a fight—says a lot for Florence Hall's cooking.

One day a prisoner, watching Sandra from the window, tossed her a quarter. "I've got an awful pain in my back. Could you get me some rubbing alcohol so I could massage it?" Sandra did as she was asked. Later when her father came home and checked on the prisoners, he found an empty alcohol bottle and the prisoner passed out drunk. Sure enough, he was feeling no pain.

Sandra, her cousin, and her friends loved to play upstairs in the cells when there were no prisoners. One thing they liked to do was to climb on top of the high security cell that had a solid steel top. They tried to read what prisoners had written up there, but they didn't know some of the words. Even when they did have prisoners, if they weren't violent, Sandra and her cousin would take a record player upstairs and sing and dance to entertain them.

She remembers one woman, who was being held there while waiting to be transported to the state hospital. The woman seemed nice, and would play cards with her through the bars. It did seem odd though that she would look out the window at the courthouse and sing to the star on it.

After a newer jail replaced this one, the Chamber of Commerce started restoration with a grant in 1979. The facility and first floor exhibits have continually been kept up. The upstairs has stayed much as the original, and visitors will find it less than a block from the square.

For information about visiting times or tours, contact: Hood County Jail Museum, 208 N. Crockett, Granbury, TX 76048 (817) 573-5135.

*Hood County Jail current appearance.*

*The old Hamilton County Jail circa 1877 from which a mob took an alleged horse thief and lynched him. Now gone. Courtesy of the Hamilton County Museum.*

# Hamilton
# Hamilton County Jail
## (1938-1990)
## Hamilton County Museum

The 1938 Hamilton County Jail is the only one I encountered done in art deco style, reflective of its era. The exterior shows it in simple lines with filigree panels where you might expect bars. On entering the former jailer's family quarters, you see plastered arches curving gracefully over the doorways.

Frank Sprague, President of the local Historical Commission, and Francis Gardner, Museum President, showed us through the building.

Exhibits are artfully arranged in the two bedrooms, one for period costumes and implements and the other for war relics. The front rooms, including the former sheriff's office, and later dispatcher's station, display historical firearms and tools.

But the Historical Commission and the museum plan to continually upgrade exhibits in a way that gives visitors a real understanding of the artifacts. Gardner indicated that several mannequins already on hand will play a part in interpretive displays. "People fifty years from now," Sprague observed, "may not have a clue how these implements were used, what life was like, or what it meant to be in jail here."

Tranquil architectural lines vanish starting at the jail stairway, which was originally blocked off from the family home. Nevertheless, by this time period the cells upstairs exemplify a gentler trend toward prisoner treatment. Only one block of cells are the woven steel cages so prevalent in older jails. The Hamilton County Jail's cells are roomier and have private shower stalls. Some cells look almost like normal rooms, having solid walls and doors, with communication ports in them. They even have exterior windows. These were possibly cells for women prisoners. Visitors will notice the plural as opposed to the usual single cell necessary for women in older jails. A nicer cell was small comfort for some, however. One young woman, arrested on drug charges, hanged herself in her cell.

Another hanging occurred in the previous jail in 1877 when a horse thief was condemned. Remember that owning a horse in the early days might be a matter of survival, so this was a serious crime. A vigilante group rode into town at night, warning citizens not involved to stay indoors. They broke the horse thief out of jail, took him to the cemetery, and lynched him from a tree. The jailer's comment of record was, "I wouldn't shoot a friend of mine to save a horse thief."

Improved law enforcement facilities and attitude should have resigned later prisoners to serve their time without disruption. But some will risk everything to get out, despite the difficulty. Several innovations were included in this jail to deter escapes. A lock-down device can still be seen in the sheriff's office. The bars were designed to foil hacksaws by inserting a separate rod inside the outer sheath that would rotate unharmed under the teeth of a saw blade. Still different attempts and successes happened.

The person to talk to about the jail is Chief Deputy Johnny Slough, who has served with the last four sheriffs. In fact Johnny and his wife Carla were the last live-in jailers. He said the only way to get a day off was to leave town where no one could call them.

One time they had done just that, and whoever was standing in for them locked up a new prisoner in the cell with a trustee, who was the only other prisoner there. Once the Sloughs came home, Johnny left to make his rounds. Carla went upstairs to take the prisoners their food. The normal procedure would have been to unlock the trustee's cell and let him deliver plates to the other prisoners. But in this situation, the violent new inmate pushed his way out and knocked her down. The trustee tried to stop him but fell and broke his arm. The bad guy, we'll call him Joe, ran downstairs, but Carla was able to lock the security doors. Trapped in the jailer's quarters, he went in the kitchen and got a knife about the time Johnny came in the front door. The two struggled and, although Johnny got cut up, he managed to get a shot off. The bullet missed "Joe" but hit the door, and the prisoner was able to get out.

Chance was not on his side though. A bottle thrown in the yard carelessly had broken, and "Joe" ran right through the shards. His feet were sliced so badly he had to give himself up and be taken to the hospital.

"Joe" wasn't the only one. Besides Johnny with his knife wounds, Carla was in shock. Imagine hearing the struggle, a shot, and fearing for your husband's life. Johnny said he decided then and there, "She didn't sign on for this job. I did. We moved out of the jail after that, and nobody else ever moved back in."

Soon afterwards, Betty Allen was one of the jailer-dispatchers who worked at the jail in shifts. She, like Deputy Slough, still works in the Sheriff's Department, but out of the new jail on the edge of town. She recalls the days when people used to walk into the old jail office any time they wanted to visit. Youngsters would talk out their problems. One guy, who roamed the town at all hours "adopted" her and would come in, sometimes in the middle of the night, to be sure she was okay. Deputy Slough remembers that guy as "deranged" but generally harmless. Apparently, that was a good thing since he was huge. Deputy Slough, six-feet-two himself, says the guy towered over him.

When asked about other jail breaks, Deputy Slough told two stories. A prisoner from out of state had been delivered to the jail for safe keeping, but the judge wasn't due in town for a long time. One night the (unnamed) sheriff told the prisoner, "Your car's outside, the doors are unlocked, and I'm going to bed. Get out of my county or be filed on for escaping." The sheriff had barely dozed off when the guy knocked on the door. His battery was dead, and he needed a jump start.

Another time a prisoner broke loose at the courthouse and ran out with officers chasing him. Former Sheriff Woodrow Young, who happened to be in the parking lot, reached into his pickup, got a rope, and lassoed him.

At the other extreme of these wannabe escape artists was the inmate who stayed there for fifteen years. By all accounts the man was smart and "could build anything" while he was within the walls of the jail. He just couldn't handle life on the outside. Eventually he was transferred to the State Hospital in Austin.

The art deco building at Hamilton provides a transition example from the very old jails to those built in the late twentieth century. As for the museum, it can take you through pioneer days up through the 1930s.

The jail museum is a block from the northwest corner of the square at 113 West Henry Street. For information about visiting times or tours, contact: Hamilton County Museum, P.O. Box 106, Hamilton, TX 76531

*Hamilton County Jail current appearance.*

*Old Helena Courthouse Square, scene of sesquicentennial festivities. Photo by Joe Baker, courtesy of* The Countywide.

# Helena
# Karnes County's First Jail
## (1854-1893)
### Ghost Town with Historical Museum

It's a ghost town now, the town called "Hell-ena." Cause of death? Possibly the attitude of being "the toughest town on earth" finally caught up with it. A variety of stories make the death sentence a mystery to this day, but no one denies it happened almost overnight.

More than twenty-five buildings, that look like a movie set for a shoot-'em-up western, stand empty except for the modern-day visitors who stop to look and wonder where everybody went. Two hotels, a string of store-fronts, and a few fine homes tell you it was obviously an important town, situated as a major stop on a well-traveled road between San Antonio and Goliad. But if this were like the movies, where was the town-taming (and bullet-proof) sheriff when they needed him? On at least two occasions, the mayhem got so bad the Texas Rangers had to be called in.

Oddly enough, out of the thirteen saloons Helena had, only the wall of one of them was still standing when I visited there. Thirteen, for a population of three to five hundred? Well, there were the cowhands who came in for a Saturday night binge, and also the shady characters and outright criminals who could find a haven here. Good citizens tried to petition the state legislature to issue an ordinance against liquor sales in the town, but their efforts failed.

The large white courthouse on the square provides a diverse and very good museum. The only thing left of the jail is the sobering sight of one iron cage, barely tall enough for a man to stand up in. Four of these cages originally sat in first a wooden building and then a two-story stone one, both of which were torn down for their materials. We don't know much about the jails but the events that happened in Helena speak volumes about how busy the jail must have been.

There were range wars, complete with the cutting of barbed wire. There was the Cart War, when ox-cart teamsters hauling goods from the coast resented the Mexicans for doing the job cheaper and faster (the teamsters dealt with their competition by destroying the Mexicans' carts and killing the drivers). This was one of the times the Rangers were called in. There was the "pastime" of the infamous Helena Duel, in which two men, tied together by one arm each, battled with short-bladed knives too short to strike a vital organ, until one or both of them bled to death.

Most residents such as the town's founders, Thomas Ruckman and Dr. Lewis Owings, who later became the governor of the Arizona Territory, had good intentions for the town, but circumstances stacked up against them. Even for volatile times, the bad guys of Helena outdid themselves. *Home & Garden TV* featured Helena as a historic landmark. *The San Antonio Daily Express* (San Antonio being no haven of peace itself) called Helena's 1884 shoot-out "one of the bloodiest street encounters we have heard of for many long days." *True West* magazine (April 1995) wrote about "The Toughest Town on Earth" and the TV program *Death Valley Days* dramatized the possible theories for why the railroad company bypassed this major town, thus diverting its financial success and county seat position to another town, which in effect, nailed down Helena's coffin.

So what were these theories? Version one: after Emmet Butler, son of wealthy rancher William Butler, was murdered in Helena, and no one would 'fess up to the deed, Butler vowed, "I'll kill the town that killed my son!" Then he exacted his revenge by contacting the railroad and donating right of way across his own land. Version two and three: for one reason or the other, both Sheriff Edgar Leary and Emmet Butler were killed in a gunfight. Version four: the railroad company required Helena, not only to donate land, which they had agreed to do, but also to pay the company a large sum of money if they wanted the tracks to come through town. Most citizens refused to pay the additional money, believing the railroad would have no choice but to go through the most important town. The railroad called Helena's bluff and accepted Mr. Butler's offer. Whether he did it for revenge or for a good business deal is still up for debate.

Shortly after the railway created a new form of transportation, the ox-cart trail closed. In 1894 the county seat was moved to Karnes City, taking most businesses with it. The jail's cages and prisoners were moved to a new county jail in Karnes City. Since that particular kind of cage had to be moved intact (see "riveted strap-iron cell construction" in Glossary), the very walls probably had to be knocked down to get the iron cells out. This would explain why there is no jail building left in Helena, and the building stone would have been too valuable not to be used elsewhere.

Karnes County Historical Society owns and maintains the village, and they host various seasonal events on the site.

For information about visiting times or tours, contact: Karnes County Historical Society, P.O. Box 162, Karnes City, TX 78118. (830) 780-3210 or visit their website at: www.accd.edu/pac/history/rhines/StudentProjects/2001/Helena/Helena.htm

*Current appearance of the last cell from the demolished jail.*

*Clay County Jail circa 1890. Courtesy of the Clay County Historical Society.*

# Henrietta
# Clay County Jail
# (1890-1973)

## Clay County Jail Museum
## & Heritage Center

The impression of Clay County Jail as a split personality building struck me at first sight with its contrasting roof lines. The genteel, Victorian half, two stories high, was the sheriff's living quarters. The other side, barred and forbidding, is three stories high with a turreted roof.

Clay County was organized in 1860, only fifteen years after Texas had joined the United States. Having 109 residents made Henrietta the most important town in the area and it, therefore, became the county seat. When the Civil War pulled troops from frontier forts, Indian raids made it impossible to maintain the town, which disbanded in 1862. Not until the 1870s did citizens reclaim it from the Kiowas. At that time the duty of providing jurisdiction over all unorganized territories west to the New Mexico border fell to Clay County, and two different jails had been built and outgrown before this one was erected in 1890.

By then Henrietta had a population of 2,100 and possessed a 400-seat opera house, a school, hotels—and several saloons. Therefore, even though its jurisdictional territory had shrunken, it needed a sizable jail. The main prisoners were "drunk cowboys, fence-cutters, claim jumpers, and cattle or chicken thieves," said historian Lucille Glasgow.

On the porch are two doors. From the wooden door of their home, the sheriff's wife would hand her husband the large, heavy keys so he could unlock the barred and steel plate door into the jail foyer. There the sheriff would book his prisoner and lock him up. Today when you enter the jail side, a hanging mannequin greets you, drawing your gaze up to the gallows and a barred skylight. A railed walkway around the second floor cells has a gate through which a condemned man could walk out on a plank extended across the open space, but no one was ever strung up there. A tree still standing on a hill near the Rodeo Ground did that job at least once.

The more private cells were used for women, juveniles, and in prohibition days, confiscated whiskey stored as evidence. One cell held long-duration prisoners, and it had a bathtub. Prominent citizens stayed there when they needed to sober up apart from common drunks. Also a well-known bootlegger once stayed there, with his own bed and other comforts moved in.

The foyer serves today as the museum office and gift shop. There visitors will see an open slot in the wall where the jailer's wife would pass through trays of food for the prisoners. The jailer used a dumb waiter to carry trays for the upper cells.

The main part of the jail was designed to house a hundred prisoners in three stacks of steel, cage-like cells. It had the usual walkways around them and one larger "drunk tank" for non-violent prisoners. The third level cells were never installed, so today it's a storage area for archives with special climate controls.

The building has the mixed blessing of sitting on top of an underground spring. Originally a windmill pumped water to huge storage tanks, thus providing running water to at least the sheriff's home, a convenience in the vanguard of its time. The other side of this blessing, however, has been the constant problem of "rising damp" undermining the building's stability. Unfortunately, some of the "fixes" made the deterioration worse. One day a section of the concrete floor gave way and dropped a lawman and prisoner. Evidence of the patched floor is still visible in the foyer.

This jail was state-of-the-art at the time it was built, even boasting steam heat with a boiler in the basement. On both floors, notice the decorative grills over the vents at the corners. But as in every jail, the prisoners' worst enemies were often themselves.

Once a woman prisoner jerked loose the gas line from her heater. The gas leak could not be repaired until morning, so the on-duty deputy had to shut off the main gas line. All prisoners had to shiver through the cold winter night along with the one who had caused the problem. In another case, a male prisoner, figuratively "soaked" with booze, tore loose a commode, soaking himself literally and as a result, almost died of pneumonia.

Prisoners used to visit relatives and friends through the barred outside windows, but to stop the exchange of contraband items, heavy metal screens had to be erected. Improvements were constantly being made, such as new first floor cells installed in 1927. Notice the saw-proof round bars compared with the flat bars of the 1890 second level cells and the lever system that opens or closes all doors in a cell block simultaneously. Despite all safeguards though, this facility had its share of jail breaks and attempts.

One prisoner escaped by using a loop of wire on a broom handle to reach the lever that opened the cells. Two other times prisoners dug through the outside wall. The story goes that one hefty guy had to be greased with lard to get him through.

The most ambitious attempt involved several prisoners. Required to clean their own cells and the holding area, this particular group seemed to be doing an outstanding job, to judge by the generous amount of dirt each man handed to the jailer. They had been flushing an even more generous amount down the toilet since they had been spending their nights tunneling through the soft brick floor. A snitch blew the whistle on the operation before it was completed, and a metal floor was installed to prevent a similar happening. One can only wonder if any of these industrious prisoners carried over their new-found cleaning skills to an honest occupation.

The museum staff has left one cell starkly bare, as a prisoner would have encountered it, a reminder that the jail was not intended for the pleasurable visit we enjoy today. History lives in comprehensively displayed exhibits in the rest of the cells and in the home section. Tributes to Native Americans, especially Chief Quanah Parker, are also found in the museum.

Former sheriffs are also fittingly memorialized. One was even immortalized in *True West* when the magazine reported the story of how Sheriff

Cooper Wright (tenure 1883-1894) single-handedly dispersed a mob trying to break a prisoner out of jail to lynch him. They didn't succeed.

But history here is neither static nor for celebrities alone. The museum staff collects stories and photos from area families not necessarily connected with the jail, and a history honoring war veterans is on-going.

As you cross the foyer from the jail through a metal door, a separate world welcomes you into a lifestyle of grace and beauty. Tall arched windows and elaborate woodwork are typical of a fine Victorian home. The décor throughout utilizes donated furnishings, artfully arranged. Every detail is itself a museum piece, some from previous occupants of the sheriff's home. Even the wallpaper was matched as closely to the original as possible.

Carma Healer, daughter of Former Sheriff Raymond Bray, lived in the beautiful quarters when she was eleven to twelve years old, and her mother taught her to cook for the prisoners. "I guess you could say, that was part of their penalty," she laughed.

Common household items not only instruct visitors on what life was like in those days, but also give tourists the feeling that a family still lives there. My favorite part of the house is the restored staircase, the three bedrooms (including collections of vintage toys and dolls), and the bathroom. Lucille Glasgow, our guide, said that displays will constantly change and grow, which makes the Museum worthy of repeat visits. The split personality of the Clay County Jail might remind you of good and evil, but here "good" has extended its way throughout the historic structure.

Clay County Jail Museum-Heritage Center is located one block west of the courthouse square. For information about special events, visiting times, or tours, contact: Clay County Historical Society, P.O. Box 483, Henrietta, TX 76565. (940) 538-5655, (940) 524-3465 or e-mail Cmuseum@wf.quik.com

*Clay County Jail current appearance.*

*Photo of the original cell moved to the Billy the Kid Museum.*

# Hico
# Hico City Jail
## (1856-1928)
### Jailhouse Library

" Step up to the bar and order a sarsaparilla," says one of Hico's brochures. It goes on to offer a $10,000 reward "payable to anyone proving Brushy Bill Roberts and Billy the Kid were not the same."

The first mystery was to find the Jailhouse Library, a stone building situated away from the downtown area and facing an alley, but it was worth the effort. Loveda Brown, the librarian, had it stocked neatly, it's air-conditioned, and there's evidence that it's doing a good job of serving the town in its more peaceful capacity. The front part, where the books are, had been the sheriff's office. Prisoners were locked in a large, attached room, separated from the front by a wooden door sheathed in decorative pressed tin. The same tin covered all but one wall of the jail room, not much of a deterrent to prisoners who wanted to pull back the tin and chisel their way through mortar between stones. But higher risk prisoners were held in an iron cage. The cell had been moved to the new city hall when it took over the job of detention from 1928 to 1964. That same riveted strap-iron cell is now at the Billy the Kid Museum downtown.

Coolidge Wade, a long-time Hico resident, told of the many uses the old jailhouse has served. It was once a cannon factory, women sewed clothing there during wartime, and it headquartered the WPA. In more recent years, it has hosted community meetings.

Talk turned to Hico's much advertised legend that the man shot down in New Mexico as Billy the Kid in 1881 had been the wrong man. The real Billy, alias Ollie (Brushy Bill) Roberts, supposedly lived to be almost ninety-one before dying peacefully. Coolidge Wade said he knew Roberts well from driving him to church. "I don't believe he was Billy the Kid, but most folks around here think that's unpatriotic." A woman who did believe it (name withheld by request) told me when she was a child, her mother made her run away when she saw Roberts "because he's crazy and dangerous."

I needed to see the jail cage and hear the pro side of the argument, so Don and I went to the Billy the Kid Museum, gift shop, and sarsaparilla bar. The steel cage is there all right, solid as ever, though its top was lost in one of the moves. The museum walls are lined with documentation and news clippings that support and explain the legend. Or if you want the documentation put together for you, there are books for sale so you can be the judge. What impressed me most is that the museum is run by the Hico Historical Society. Jane Klein and Marguerite Thomas, both Historical Society members, showed us through the exhibit, pointing out key evidence.

Here's the claim. In the 1881 gunfight we've always heard about at Lincoln County, New Mexico, Pat Garrett supposedly shot, not Billy the Kid, but Billy Barlow by mistake. The real one, merely wounded, escaped and made his way into Mexico. Descriptions conflicted. The Las Vegas, New Mexico *Gazette*, that interviewed William Bonney aka Billy the Kid only a few months before, described him as "a mere boy," with silky fuzz on his upper lip. The *Grant County Herald* obituary described the corpse as having a full beard. Nevertheless, Garrett collected the $500 reward for capturing Billy and wrote his book, *The Authentic Life of Billy the Kid.*

Under different aliases, the Kid supposedly surfaced several times: riding in Buffalo Bill's Wild West Show, scouting for stage coach lines, working for Pinkerton Detective Agency, joining Teddy Roosevelt's Rough Riders, serving as deputy marshal in Oklahoma, and more.

And what about the real Ollie Roberts? Mistaken for a rustler and hanged, they say. Did Billy see this as an opportunity to take on the other man's identity?

An attorney, believing Brushy Bill to be Bonney, contacted the old man when he was almost ninety-one years old. They went to New Mexico to meet Governor Mabry requesting a pardon, but the publicity and excitement made the old man too ill to go through with it. The governor sent him back to Hico to live out his days in peace. Whoever Brushy Bill Roberts was, he died of a heart attack about a month later on his way to the Hico Post Office in December 1950.

Hico resident Bob Heffner wrote a book about the case, *The Trial of Billy the Kid.* Then he and New Mexico resident William Tunstall put their research together to validate the legend. Tunstall, who wrote *Billy the Kid and Me Were the Same,* was kin to John Tunstall, a rancher who had befriended Billy and was a player in the Lincoln County War. Later, armed with new research, Heffner collaborated with Dr. Jannay Valdez to write *Billy the Kid Killed in New Mexico—Died in Texas.*

Whenever you go to Hico, try to do it during the annual Billy the Kid Festival so you can experience the showmanship of a lively little town. Even if you don't solve the mystery and win the reward, you can at least have fun, and when you belly up to the bar for that sarsaparilla, drink an extra one for me.

Follow the signs to find the Billy the Kid Museum. There you can ask for directions to the Library. For information about visiting times or tours, contact: Billy the Kid Museum, North Pecan St., Hico, TX 76457. (254) 796-4004. For the Jailhouse Library, c/o Chamber of Commerce, P.O. Box 561, Hico, TX 76457. (254) 796-4285 or (254) 796-2523 or visit their website at: www.hico-tx.com

*Hico City Jail current appearance.*

## Kirbyville
# Kirbyville City Jail in Jasper County
## (1910-1954)
### Calaboose Museum

Kirbyville is a town that lumber built in 1895, a "company town." Its founder, John Henry Kirby, earned the sobriquet "Prince of the Pines" by producing more southern pine lumber than any other man in the region. The town is surrounded by the Big Thicket as well as state and national forests. Parts of Jasper County look as untamed as they must have appeared to Spanish and French explorers a couple of centuries before.

Not much information about the old jail is available, even to the Heritage Society that now operates a museum inside the building. It had apparently served as a satellite jail for the county of Jasper, but don't let its small size fool you into thinking it only housed the harmless. Thanks to County Judge Joe Folk's introductions, I got to talk to two former sheriffs who had used this calaboose.

Sheriff Aubrey Cole hadn't been on the job but a couple of months before he was put to the test. He had "inherited" two prisoners accused of robbery. While allowed out of their cell in the runaround, they apparently let down a string for someone on the ground to send up a hacksaw. With no jailer on the premises, the first thing Sheriff Cole knew of a jail break came from the dispatcher. One of the escapees eventually was caught in Houston and the other in California.

He says the really bad prisoners seemed to come all at once, like the time they had five women murderers in one year. Another time he had a jail full of unusually mean male inmates. One of them called to the deputy that he needed something for a stomach-ache. When the deputy took the medicine upstairs, a prisoner hit him over the head. The deputy never recovered and later died from the injury.

The second floor of the Kirbyville jail has a free-standing, barred cell and two other rooms with solid, two-foot-thick walls. These were used either for solitary confinement or to keep women prisoners separate. Cole says that, to his knowledge, no jailer ever lived in the building, and the first floor also was used for prisoners.

Cole wrote a column each week for the newspaper, and once his young deputy gave him a particularly good subject to write about. Both of them had gone into an empty cell with the door propped open. The prop accidentally got kicked aside, the door slammed—they were locked in until somebody came and found them. That deputy's name was Joe Folk, none other than the current county judge who referred me to the two sheriffs.

Cole might have continued as sheriff except for the fact that he needed to care for his aging father, and was never home to do it. With eighteen months remaining in his term, Deputy Folk agreed to serve out the term for him as sheriff. Folk did not seek re-election as sheriff, but instead ran for County Judge, an office he has held ever since. Cole says, "He's a better judge than sheriff—too kind-hearted."

When Thomas Nixon got back from the Army, he started his career in law enforcement as Chief of Police for the City of Jasper before being elected county sheriff. The worst murder cases he dealt with were a shootout leaving one man dead, and a man having his throat cut and landing with both armpits stuck on a picket fence. To Nixon's frustration, neither arrest resulted in a conviction. Even more frustrating, he says, was the trouble with drunks and dope users that "never seemed to do any good." As for his overall view of the job, he says, "I treated people the way I wanted to be treated."

By 1954, the old jail could no longer meet the state's penal standards. Also, due to better roads and transportation, satellite jails had outlived their usefulness, so the Kirbyville City Jail was shut down. The Kirbyville Area Heritage Society agreed to turn the jail into the Calaboose Museum. While visitors may first be attracted by their curiosity to see inside a jail, they stay to look at the attractive displays downstairs.

The curator once told me, "The exhibits reflect slices of life throughout Kirbyville's history. A significant portion of the wall space is dedicated to photos of earlier days and well known people of bygone eras. These are expanded upon in the many photo albums available to browse through. Other displays show physician's tools and pharmacists products from earlier times, century-old clothes, artifacts from the early days of the Santa Fe Depot, and other signs of times past."

The Calaboose is located at Elizabeth and Lavielle Streets. For information about visiting times or tours, contact: Kirbyville Area Heritage Society, P.O. Box 100, Kirbyville, TX 75956. Also Chamber of Commerce Office, 105 S. Elizabeth, Kirbyville, TX 75956. (409) 423-5827.

*Kirbyville City Jail. Courtesy of the Kirbyville Calaboose Museum.*

*A detailed photograph of one of the displays found in the museum. Courtesy of the Calaboose Museum.*

*Fayette County Jail. Courtesy of the Fayette County Old Jail Cultural Council, Inc.*

# La Grange
# Fayette County Jail
# (1883-1985)

## Chamber of Commerce/Visitor Center/Museum

Don't let the serene, church-like appearance of the Fayette County Jail fool you. Prisoners had anything but a heavenly life there. Not that the jailers were cruel, just stern and efficient. Hardship was a way of life for the jailer and his family, who made their home in the jail.

Two meals each day consisted of cornbread and molasses with the possible addition of a small piece of meat and a carrot, plus a half cup of coffee in the morning. Inmates shared a common basin for both drinking water and washing, so illness was common.

Still this facility must have seemed luxurious compared to what had gone before. The first jail only cost $460 to build, and the county officials sold it after ten years. Prisoners were ironed, chained, and farmed out to local citizens for labor. Hardened criminals were transported to another county until 1854 when Fayette County built another jail. Nevertheless, by the early 1880s a better facility was needed. They started with a basement, housing prisoners below ground while construction of the magnificent two-story structure was being completed.

Each floor held eight cells with space for four or five prisoners. The jailer had to check on prisoner disturbances no matter when they occurred, day or night. But to do so was both annoying and potentially dangerous. One jailer came up with a clever solution. A series of anomalies in the walls, now handsomely plastered, look like round bathroom basins turned on their sides, complete with what appears to be a center drain. These are peep holes, strategically placed in the thick walls so the jailer could view any part of the cell blocks.

Improvements made in 1884 included hiring a prison guard to help the sheriff, building a tall iron fence, and installing indoor plumbing. Up to that time, prisoners had been escorted once a day to carry their own buckets to the outhouse.

One of two "hoosegows" or "calabooses" still stands on the grounds. It gave ordinary citizens a chance to repent getting drunk without having to share cell-space with criminals. But the tin-roofed windowless shed must have made quite a hot box by morning.

One item on exhibit at the museum is a diagram for a scaffold, only the foundation of which remains. The scaffold was built under the strict supervision of Sheriff August Loessin (tenure 1895-1920), who took great care to do the job as humanely as possible. Details also specified that the hangman's rope should be tied at the top with an unlucky thirteen wraps, and six wraps for the knot in the noose, supposedly signifying the Devil whom the prisoner was going to meet.

One of the jail's most grisly events involved a flood and no one could have prevented what happened. Before the Lower Colorado River Authority built dams for flood control in the 1940s, the first clue of a flood was likely to be a wall of water rolling down the river bed like a tidal wave, and folks were lucky if they could save themselves. Several floods roared through the town from the 1860s to the 1900s.

Director of Tourism, Cathy Chaloupka, suggested that I look beneath what had formerly been the Sheriff's interview room. Outside I peered through those barred windows only to find that dirt fills the space almost to ground level. One flood had made a sudden deposit of sediment. No record tells the year of the flood or the fate of prisoners stranded in that basement. We can only imagine.

Not all prisoners were males, so the jail had a women's cell, too, smaller and apart from the others. A discreet potty chair made to look like an ordinary straight chair now sits outside the women's cell for the purpose of museum display.

The first woman in Texas ever to be sentenced for execution spent her last days in the Fayette County Jail. Her name was Mary (or Marie) Dach. A play-by-play story of the investigation appeared in the June 1935 issue of *Famous Detective Cases*. The article, "The Fantastic Tale of Widow Dach," by B. Mattingly was told by Chief Deputy Jim Flournoy, who had helped Sheriff William Loessin solve the murder case.

Nut-shelled, here's the story. Mary Dach's husband had died, leaving her with a farm to manage and three small children to bring up. Though quite robust, or as Deputy Flournoy said, "Herculean," this woman hired a live-in farmhand, Henry Stoever. Apparently, Stoever proved abusive to Mrs. Dach and her children, but she couldn't get him to leave.

Stoever's family seldom saw him and didn't notice when he went missing. Only a series of letters, supposedly written by Stoever to his daughter, finally roused them two months later to report his suspicious absence. Mrs. Dach, a German barely literate in English, had crudely forged these letters, the first written well before Stoever's disappearance. The daughter and her husband had not questioned that Stoever wrote the letters despite several questionable aspects. He addressed them as "Der Dotter and Brother in Law" rather than by name, explained signing over $548 worth of notes to the Widow Dach, and claimed he was dying from cancer (as Mrs. Dach's husband had). Further, the letter said he intended to end it all in the Columbia River (meaning the Colorado).

Sheriff Loessin and Deputy Flournoy got conflicting stories from Dach about where the farmhand had gone. Signs of recently turned earth made Loessin suspicious, so using a sharpened wagon rod normally used to search for illegal liquor, he found the covered excavation to be about six by three feet.

Under charred timbers, they uncovered the remains of a human body, including one side of the face and red-haired scalp. Mrs. Dach at first claimed it was a dead calf, but at last, she admitted it was Stoever, who had shot himself. She had dumped him in the hole he himself had dug for a different purpose. She insisted that she only burned and buried him for fear of spreading the cancer.

Eventually she confessed to shooting him in his sleep to stop his abusiveness and get rid of him. Her earlier forged letters, however, accounting for how she came to have Stoever's money indicated an additional motive.

After being sentenced to die in the electric chair, she refused to eat, determined to "cheat the chair." At one point, she hallucinated that the chair in her cell was the one she dreaded. She eventually died of starvation.

An avid historian and genealogist, Cathy Chaloupka is writing a book she's titled *Unsettled Spirits around La Grange*, which includes stories from the Fayette County Jail. She says she isn't the only one who has sensed, heard, and seen plenty of paranormal happenings in the area formerly occupied by Mrs. Dach's cell. "Can you name a place more likely?" she asks.

Most prisoners, of course, exited with body and soul still intact.

The most notorious inmates were two members of the Bonnie and Clyde gang during the mid-1930s. Raymond Hamilton and Gene O'Dare were being held in the jail until federal officers arrived. Fearing a breakout situation, the sheriff stationed shotgun-armed men around the tall iron fence, waiting to fend off Bonnie and Clyde. Fortunately, they never showed up. The handsome Hamilton had plenty of other visitors though. Women from miles around brought him cookies, cakes, and pies just to have a look at him.

Any account of legal doings in La Grange would be incomplete without mentioning the "Chicken Ranch," made famous by the Broadway play and later movie, *The Best Little Whorehouse in Texas*. Sheriff Jim Flournoy, portrayed in the story as the establishment's best customer, was by all accounts, instead a happily married man. Practicality guided him to allow the business to operate because it did so discreetly while benefiting local hotels, restaurants, and gasoline stations. Flournoy's long tenure, first as a Deputy and then as Sheriff from 1947-1980 indicates the townspeople's approval. His portrait and those of other sheriffs grace the walls of the museum room today.

The county has taken great pride that no prisoner ever escaped. A few years ago, a Houston radio station reported a prisoner escaping from the prison at Huntsville. The reporter noted that the last time it had happened was when a member of the Bonnie and Clyde gang escaped after being *successfully* held in the Fayette County Jail.

After serving as a jail for more than a hundred years, the Victorian Gothic building was retired in 1985. The Fayette County Commissioners, the Cultural Council, and the La Grange Area Chamber of Commerce cooperated to renovate and restore the jail.

Because of its current use as Chamber offices, the old jail is open to visitors every day, and the first floor holding area is now a meeting room and museum. For information about visiting times or tours, contact: Chamber of Commerce, 171 South Main, La Grange, TX 78945. (979) 968-5756 or visit their website at: www.lagrangetx.org

Originally published in *American Jails* magazine as "Jails Have Come a Long Way, Baby!" January/February 2005. Reprinted with permission of the American Jail Association.

*Fayette County Jail current appearance.*

# Llano
# Llano County Jail
## (1895-1981)
### Old Red Top

Llano never had a respectable jail before "Old Red Top" was built in 1895, and before construction of the jail was completed the county's hangings took place on an oak tree at the present intersection of Highway 16 and Main Street. The decision to locate the jail away from the courthouse seems odd unless you consider the hoosegows that preceded it.

According to Pamela Fowler's booklet *The Red Top*, records are unclear about the nature of the jail built in the 1870s, but in 1881 the notation that they sold its iron roofing indicates there was one. Before the county could get the new jail erected, lawmen incarcerated their felons in the basement of a two-story building a block north of the square, with guards hired to watch the doors. Outside was an iron grate for ventilation, and author Wilburn Oatman, in his book *Llano, Gem of the Hill Country*, recounts that when he was twelve or thirteen in 1881 or 1882, the town boys interacted with prisoners through the grate. What he and his friends learned there no doubt offset the proper upbringing they received at home and school. On one occasion, the basement "guests" performed a mock trial for the boys' entertainment. The leader of the group played the prosecuting attorney, and the jury ultimately found the defendant guilty of stealing hogs.

Around that time Judge John Oatman, Wilburn's elder, was presenting plans to the commissioners' court for a new calaboose, and in 1882, it was constructed about where the World War I monument now stands. The stone building had a jailer's residence on the ground floor and a dungeon underneath containing an iron cage. Sanitation must have been a problem, but it was 1890 before the county installed sewer pipes from the jailhouse to empty into the Llano River. A cowpen next to the jail yard further worsened the situation. In 1894 the city condemned it as a public nuisance, and furthermore demanded that the next jail be constructed a good distance from the public square.

Little did they know what a beauty Red Top would be, "affectionately" nicknamed by prisoners for its original red painted roof. Apparently the county had become wealthy enough by that time to build not only the sizable gray granite prison, but also the current courthouse two years before, in Romanesque Revival style, three stories high plus a hanging tower with cupola. The first floor furnished the sheriff's living quarters, typical and of a generous size. There are three rooms with fireplaces and the kitchen, not counting the entry room where prisoners were brought in, processed, and then escorted upstairs. Perhaps it was this ample space that prompted one sheriff to rent out part of it, until the county told him he had to stop.

Two levels of cell-blocks surround steel stairways, and in the center of the three levels is the opening for the hanging gallows in the tower. Prisoners whose cells faced it had this long drop to consider at all times. When Cheryl Crabtree of the Chamber of Commerce showed us through, looking up into that hole certainly gave me a chill. The gallows never served for a hanging, but at various times it did serve as an escape route for prisoners to climb into the gallows and through that tallest section of roof. The practice came to a halt when a locked steel door was installed and the hinged trapdoor welded shut. After hanging as a method of execution was discontinued in Texas, the trapdoor was no longer needed anyway. Besides, there was always that certain tree.

About 1981, the state declared certain standards for modern jails, and Old Red Top had to be closed down. Prisoners were sent to the lockup in Brady while the current jail was being completed.

For quite some time, the county's Headstart school program made Red Top its headquarters. One has to wonder what effect going to jail each day had on impressionable preschoolers, but they definitely had a sturdy roof over their heads. In 1985 the local chapter of the Daughters of the Republic of Texas took over as custodians of the jail, until the job became too overwhelming with needed repairs and maintenance, and they relinquished it. Near the end of 2001, the county commissioners accepted the Llano County Historical Commission's request for a fifty-year lease of the building at $10 a year. Mainstreet Manager Sarah Oatman Franklin is currently working to obtain a grant to restore the historical building.

It is open for selected community events as listed on the website calendar (shown below), such as: Heritage Day (October), Llano Country Opry (2nd Saturdays), Rodeo (1st weekend in June), school or other group requests. Cheryl Crabtree says once when she and Sarah Franklin were downstairs, they were startled when a self-guided group shrieked and hurried downstairs. "There's a man sleeping in one of the cells!" they said.

"Oh, that's just Pedro," Crabtree said, and then explained "Pedro" is a mannequin. But I could understand the group's consternation. In the dim light of that particular cell, it was hard to tell what condition the sleeping man was in.

> The Red Top can be found across from the library just south of the river. For information about visiting times or tours, contact: Llano Chamber of Commerce, 700 Bessemer, Llano, TX 78643. (325) 247-5354 or visit their website at: www.llanochamber.org

*An "inspiring" view up to the gallows from cells facing the stairwell.*

*Llano County Jail current appearance.*

# Lockhart
# Caldwell County Jail
## (1909-1983)
### Caldwell County Museum
### and Visitor Center

Driving through Lockhart on the main highway, travelers may be surprised to see the red brick towers of a Norman castle standing taller than the buildings in front of it. "Why," many people ask, "did they build old jails to look like something out of a storybook: castles, strongholds, and fortresses with battlements?" Modern jails, substantial and functional as they are, lack such dramatic appearances. The historians I've met on this project seem to agree that people of the frontier times when most of these jails were built craved civil authority and a jail that symbolized something larger than life.

Lockhart citizens first made do with a log jail, until it burned down; second the basement of the courthouse, until it couldn't hold all the felons; and third a stone jail until they got tired of its not having necessary facilities. That last one didn't even have a gallows for the two legal hangings prescribed in its time. Executions took place outside—legal or otherwise. Rumors have it that frightful deeds happened within the walls as well. For whatever reasons, the townspeople in 1908 voted by a huge majority to tear the structure down and build a better jail. The previous one was completely dismantled and a citizen bought the stones to build his store.

The 1909 jail stands as a testament to a job done right. Three stories high, its first floor served as quarters for a jailer's family, while the second and third floors held the cells. A center tower rises even higher as a cell for the truly incorrigible. The area below it is open for the drop from the gallows, which were never used and were taken out sometime in the 1930s. Still the sight of it must have given prisoners a choking sensation.

Although there are no records to prove it, John Wesley Hardin supposedly spent time in this jail. Another undocumented story tells of a jail break in which one skinny prisoner escaped through the dumbwaiter shaft, ordinarily used for food to be carried upstairs. If it did happen, he would have escaped through the family quarters. That the dumbwaiter is welded shut these days gives credence to the tale.

Official records or not, prisoners kept their own journals of sorts. Even if they didn't sign their names, they seemed to want to immortalize their thoughts on the walls. Their graffiti has outlasted them in such sayings as, "Mae West forever," "Witch's workshop," and "I never picked up a dead man's gun."

About the time the 1909 jail was opened for business, Sheriff J.H. Franks was elected. His tenure was interrupted in 1915 when an assassin killed him. The man appointed to take over as sheriff was Walter Ellison, who held the job for the next twenty-five years.

By 1983 a new jail was built, and the Caldwell County Historical Commission obtained permission to make a museum of the old jail. The town's character greatly reflects its pioneer heritage. Exhibits are changed periodically, but the Chisholm Trail display particularly fascinated me with all its implements and clothing used by people from the area. The town celebrates Chisholm Trail Days annually, with the Old Jail, as Visitor Center, some years playing a role when they stage a "jail break."

But we need to back up to understand the importance of the trail drives to the citizens. The usual post-Civil War hardships were worsened by a severe drought, so that even established pioneers couldn't succeed at farming alone. What Texas did have plenty of were wild cattle, first brought in by early Spaniards but evolved into the tough longhorn cattle we think of today. Northern states were hungry for beef, and here was a product that could furnish its own transportation to the markets, and graze along the way. Various enterprising Texas cattle drovers found routes, including numerous feeder branches and the more westerly trails blazed by Charles Goodnight and Oliver Loving. But Lockhart's interest is in the Chisholm Trail.

Our guide, Phyllis Metcalfe, really hooked me when she said some people from other states deny that Texas was part of the Chisholm Trail at all.

Of course towns along the route, like Lockhart, will fiercely defend it as a historical fact and show evidence to prove it. As curator Donaly Brice explained, "The debate centers around who had a right to be called the namesake." Was it exclusively Jesse Chisholm? Thornton Chisholm? John Chism? Or somebody else?

Just about every historian acknowledges that Jesse Chisholm, half-Cherokee half-Scotsman, drove freight wagons through Indian Territory of Oklahoma to his trading post in Kansas in 1866, thus leaving wagon ruts for others to follow. Historian T.R. Fehrenbach even states in his book *Lone Star* that the trail started "deep in Texas." Thornton Chisholm, also in 1866, gathered a herd of longhorns near Cuero, one branch of which came through Lockhart.

A resolution to the controversy is far too complicated to be settled on the pages of this book, but any sleuth is welcome to try, and an interesting way to start is to visit museums along the way that have physical evidence and traditional stories. These tales come from the memories of cowboys, whose cattle drives took the better part of a year, and from hapless settlers, whose fences and gardens were flattened by several thousand longhorns on the move. Would so many people have imagined this? As for a disparity of exactly where the trails went, keep in mind that several herds would require space miles wide, and would need to move over to find ungrazed land for "fuel." A most helpful and objective website is: www.thechisholmtrail.com

The jail in Lockhart is not short on stories. Here's another sort of mystery. Persistent rumors of ghosts attracted a group out of San Antonio, the Alamo City Paranormal Investigators, to gather evidence of what visitors claim to sense at the jail. Tape recordings picked up the kind of sounds that skeptics attribute to "any old building," but where did that gunshot come from? As it turns out, ordinary people have also asked about that sound. Although the investigators didn't see anything, their cameras picked up some unexplainable anomalies. Editor's note: Shelley Andrews wrote a whole chapter about this aspect of the Lockhart Jail in *Ghostly Tales from America's Jails,* and you may check out the paranormal investigators' website at: www.lonestarspirits.org

Whether or not you believe these stories, a tour of the jail will be interesting.

Look for the Norman castle one block east of Highway 183 at 315 East Market St. For information about visiting times or tours, contact: Caldwell County Museum, P.O. Box 297, Lockhart, TX 78644. (512) 398-5879 or visit their website at: www.lockhart-tx.org

*Caldwell County Jail current appearance.*

*An interior photograph of the top floor of the Caldwell County Jail.*

*A photograph of the Old Mobeetie Jail.*

# Mobeetie
# Wheeler County Jail
## (1886-1907)
### Mobeetie Jail Museum

Mobeetie has had several names, the most important being "Mother City of the Panhandle." The only settlement in that vast region in 1874, it started as a simple camp called "Hidetown" where buffalo hunters gathered. Few other Caucasians risked a trip through the area for fear of Indian attacks.

The deadly Apaches had been ousted by the deadlier Kiowas and Comanches, who didn't welcome the westward movement of "Americans." The Red River War of 1874 defeated the Indians and cleared the way for white settlers. That called for U.S. cavalry and infantry to keep the conquered tribes in the Indian Territory of Oklahoma, so in 1875 Fort Elliott was set up not far from the Panhandle's only town. Hidetown boomed, not only as a buying center for buffalo skins, but also for catering to the soldiers as consumers.

It soon had a Chinese laundry and several saloons, one of which served the black "buffalo soldiers" exclusively. It also had a restaurant, co-owned by Ellen O'Loughlin with her husband, and she was known as the only virtuous woman in town. Over a dozen other women residents were saloon girls. The men's major professions were bullwhackers, buffalo hunters, gamblers, and outlaws. The Goodnight/Loving Trail also went through the area, but even if the cowhands were allowed into town, they would have had no money until they got the cattle to market. Rancher and Texas Ranger Charles Goodnight said, "Mobeetie . . . was the hardest place I ever saw on the frontier except Cheyenne, Wyoming."

The town was a stop-over for the infamous as well as the famous: Bartholomew "Bat" Masterson, previously a scout in the Red River War; Pat Garrett, who was heralded as the man who shot Billy the Kid; and Poker Alice, widowed by three husbands, lucky at cards, unlucky in love. Dance hall girl, Elizabeth "Frenchy" McCormick, so called for her fluency in French, became a legend for loyalty to her undying love. About 1880 she met gambler Mickey McCormick who had a livery stable in Tascosa, a newer town as wild as Mobeetie. Mickey and Frenchy married and built a home in Tascosa, where Frenchy dealt cards in their saloon. (Tascosa today is the site of Cal Farley's Boys' Ranch.)

One of the earliest marked graves in Mobeetie's cemetery was that of Mollie Brennan dated 1876. This dance hall girl happened to get in the way during a saloon gunfight. Bat Masterson was a faro dealer at the saloon, which was owned by Henry Fleming, the county's first sheriff. Masterson and a sergeant got into an argument over the game and Mollie. They drew on each other, and the sergeant was killed. The sergeant's bullet passed through Mollie and hit Masterson in the hip. It left Masterson with a permanent limp, and Mollie dead.

Respectable settlers arrived to the area as well. In the same cemetery, another grave is that of General Sam Houston's granddaughter, Louise. She died of cholera in 1887 at the age of two.

By 1880 the need for a jail could not be denied. As the seat of Wheeler County, Mobeetie built a two-story courthouse with a jail on the top floor. George Arrington and his Texas Rangers tamed the town to some extent, and Arrington was elected sheriff in 1882. More jail space was soon needed, so the citizens built a second stone building with sheriff's quarters on the first floor and a jail on the top. Luckily they had this jail in place when a tornado destroyed the older courthouse-jail.

Sheriff Arrington and his family were the first to live in the new 1886 jail. The name "Hidetown" didn't seem to fit the community anymore, and people were calling the town "Sweetwater City" after a nearby creek.

Fort Elliott was abandoned by 1890. Its only remains are on the grounds of the Old Mobeetie Jail Museum: an strap-iron cage from the fort's jail and the original flagpole. Visitors often ask where these fifty-foot-long, straight poles were found on the panhandle plains. Surprisingly such trees were plentiful enough to have made the fort's picket-style stockade. I had to see for myself the nearby green valley carved out of the cap rock by the Canadian River.

Mobeetie suffered when the county seat was moved to Wheeler in 1907. Then in 1929, when the railroad missed it by about a mile, most of Mobeetie's residents moved to be close to the tracks and established New Mobeetie.

Of course the jail had closed when the county seat moved, and for quite some time, private citizens rented the building as a residence. Later the Veterans of Foreign Wars acquired the building, but donated it to be used as a museum and reception area when the Old Mobeetie Association organized.

Members Louise Hogan and Dale Corcoran told us that, at some point, the cells had been taken out. These cells had been on the outer edges, with a runabout around a central staircase. That staircase has been moved to the side wall. The original hanging device is still there, which could be dragged out of the way when not in use or placed over an opening to allow the trapdoor to drop a prisoner. This floor today has an impressive set of exhibits grouped to show the stages of history, with costumed mannequins for each: early Native Americans, buffalo hunters and the Wild West, Fort Elliott soldiers, and settlers.

Exhibits on the lower floor give you a feeling for pioneer life and a later, more gracious lifestyle. Some frontier scenes are displayed in a playful way, such as when you exit through a rear door, you notice a room off to the side. In it is a life-like mannequin in a bathtub. Tour guides say visitors have been known to exclaim, "Excuse me!"

At the beginning of this article, I said the town had several names through out the years. "Mobeetie," which they settled on, may have been the least fortunate. As the town became more civilized, citizens applied for a post office under the name of "Sweetwater." The state rejected the application because there was already a town by that name. Looking for a way around the technicality, city fathers asked local Indians for the native translation of the word and were told it was "mobeetie." Not until several years later did a friendly Comanche tell them the true meaning of the word was "buffalo dung." Last laugh goes to the Indians!

The museum sponsors various large events, and the seven-acre grounds have camping areas, including 136 RV hookups, a covered meeting pavilion, and public restroom facilities.

Wheeler is on U.S. Highway 183, with the "almost ghost town" of Old Mobeetie a few miles west on Highway 152. For information about visiting times or tours, contact: Old Mobeetie Association, P.O. Box 66, Mobeetie, TX 79061. (806) 845-2028 or (806) 826-3427 e-mail them at omjm@pan-tex.net or visit their website at www.mobeetie.com

*Photograph of the 1907 jail at Wheeler, now city offices.*

*A photograph of the original portable hanging device.*

# Monahans
# Ward County Jail
## (1928-1932)
### Old Hoosegow at the
### Million Barrel Museum

Ward County's first jail, undeniably humble, sits in company with the area's most grandiose project constructed during the rush for "black gold," the Million Barrel Tank. Both built about the same time, they're smack-dab in the middle of the Permian Basin sandhills. How in the world did two objects so different get together?

In 1927, an oil boom turned the tiny town of Monahans into a tent city full of roughnecks—which might explain why they soon needed a jail. Before that, the occasional law breaker was simply manacled, standing, to a pole. They built a no-frills, twelve by sixteen-foot jail of double-wall lumber. Its only ventilation was a six by thirty-inch barred window at each end. This was the only hoosegow they had for a number of years, but if it hadn't been for the tank, the simple wooden jail might never have survived after a new jail replaced it in 1932. So, what's so special about this particular tank?

Visualize an eight-acre dish sunken in the ground with thirty-foot high earthen walls, all concrete-lined. Now visualize it full of a million barrels—that's forty-five-million gallons—of crude oil. With all the drilling, companies soon had more oil than the pipelines and other transportation could carry. The over-supply had the price down to seventy-five cents a barrel. Shell Oil Company figured an enormous storage tank would pay for itself even if used only once. So they scooped out a basin with mule-drawn fresnoes (forerunners to modern bulldozer shovels).

In 1930 the tank was abandoned due to the Great Depression—not to mention the fact that the tank leaked. Fortunately by that time, the pipelines could handle the oil companies needs. The city of Monahans leased the empty structure at a dollar a year for a recreational area, frequently holding dances on the tank floor.

Since all of this occurred during the Prohibition Era, it should come as no surprise that some of the jail's patrons had something to do with bootleg whiskey. What's more unusual, a big murder case stemmed from controversy of an *inanimate* inmate locked up in the jail. Archivist Elizabeth Heath told me the story of a woman bootlegger, Lea Bailey. Bailey had a "hush money" arrangement with law officer, Dan Horn, to turn a blind eye to her operation. After a time though, Horn demanded more, so he locked the contraband liquor in the calaboose, threatening to use it as evidence against Bailey unless she agreed to his demands. She refused, and he hit her over the head. Bailey pulled out a gun and started shooting. Horn fled, but she gave chase. When he fell in front of the pool hall, she shot him five more times. Records don't report whether or not she was locked up with her liquor.

But, back to the Million-Barrel Tank. In 1958 Wayne and Amalie Long bought the tank to make a water park of it. Wayne drilled eleven water wells, but the "poor" guy struck oil in nine of them. Still he was able to fill it with water at last, and Melody Park held a Grand Opening on October 5, 1958, complete with stunt water skiers. Unfortunately, the tank proved unable to hold water any better than it had oil, and the park closed the same year.

In 1984 Amalie Long, then a widow, donated the tank to Ward County to be used in a Texas Sesquicentennial Project, and what a project it became! As a museum complex, in addition to the old jail, several other historical structures were moved in along with various accouterments and machinery. The Holman House-Hotel, built in the late 1890s and situated at the terminus of the Monahans-Grandfalls-Fort Stockton Stagecoach line, welcomed guests from that mode of travel as well as the railroad. It later served oil field personnel, and after several years, was moved to the museum site. Other buildings at the site are a caretaker's cottage, a school building, and Monahans' first depot building. The museum recently added a caboose and boxcar to go with the depot, and the retiring Southwestern Bell Telephone also contributed its building.

The tank has become the Meadows' Amphitheatre, named for its bene-factor, the Algur H. Meadows Foundation. Bleacher seats accommodate 400. The roofed stage has dressing rooms at each end.

The jail, a stark reminder of the fate early lawbreakers could expect, is the first exhibit visitors see on the left as they enter an impressive gateway. This gateway, as well as walkways and curbing, were funded by the Sid Richardson Foundation, in honor of the man who made his fortune in West Texas.

The Million Barrel Museum Complex is east of town on Highway 80/20. For information about visiting times or tours, contact: Ward County Historical Commission, 400 E. 4th Street, Monahans, TX 79756. (432) 943-8401 or visit their website at www.monahans.org/new/chamber/museums.html

*Ward County Jail current appearance. Paula Nichols photographer.*

*A photograph of the early cabins, part of the museum complex.*

## Palo Pinto
# Palo Pinto County Jail
## (1882-1941)
## Palo Pinto County Pioneer Museum

One look at Palo Pinto's frontier jail, and you know it intended serious business with no frills. It reflects the area's stern past following the South's crushing defeat in the Civil War and hard times during Reconstruction. Cowboys weren't just myth here, and nobody proved it better than rancher Oliver Loving and former Indian fighter/Texas Ranger Charles Goodnight. The two teamed up to match Texas's plentiful supply of wild longhorn cattle with the demand for beef in northern states. Near Palo Pinto in 1866, the two men opened up what was to become the Goodnight-Loving Trail. Larry McMurtry, in his Pulitzer Prize winning novel *Lonesome Dove* patterned the exploits of his Rangers, Gus and Call, after these two real-life heroes. Yes, even down to Goodnight's honoring his friend's last request to take his body home for burial.

Although the Palo Pinto Jail didn't come along until 1882, attitudes of toughness and keeping to the basics still held sway, as the sturdy, unadorned walls indicate. The portion of the ground floor allotted to living quarters for the sheriff's family consisted of only two rooms, one of which was the kitchen. Another room on that level, separated from the home by a steel door, was the sheriff's office where prisoners were brought in. Stairs in that area led to the cells on the second floor. A slot in the steel door allowed the sheriff's wife to pass food through for the sheriff to deliver to the prisoners.

Upstairs a large communal room contained iron-barred cells with some shared sanitation facilities. A separate, private cell was available for women. Bob Bellamy, our guide, shared his knowledge of county history while we toured the building. He explained that the cells in the museum today are not original to the jail. Those were removed to be used elsewhere after the jail was taken out of service. Later, the jail at Albany, which had the same floor plan as the one in Palo Pinto, sent its unwanted cells over to restore the building to its original appearance.

Completion of the courthouse, built the same year as the jail, was delayed when a tornado took off its roof, so the jail had to start off its service as a courthouse as well. However, as a jail, it held its first death-sentence prisoner in 1897. Lacking an indoor gallows, the county constructed a scaffold on the public square, with schools and businesses closed so that no one would have to miss the spectacle. One story goes that the fall through the trapdoor failed to break the man's neck. A deputy sheriff grabbed the struggling body around the waist to add the needed tug and bring the execution to a more merciful end. Five years later, a scaffold was installed inside the jail but never used, and eventually the state of Texas declared that all executions would take place at Huntsville.

By 1941, the Works in Progress Administration (WPA) built a third courthouse containing a jail and sheriff's office on the top floor. Thus the old jail was vacated and sat abandoned for almost thirty years. Only when a private citizen offered to dismantle and move the building to his property, did the citizens wake up and realize they had a perfect building for a pioneer museum. County Judge John Smith challenged the town to come up with $5,000 for a new roof and windows. A booster club temporarily spearheaded the project until the Palo Pinto County Historical Association, Inc., could be organized. Major structural repairs were undertaken and completed before exhibits could even be considered. When citizens began contributing implements and artifacts, space inside the restored jail soon filled up, and the Association turned the lot into a complex of other pioneer buildings.

Thanks to the generosity of heirs, three historical log cabins have been brought in and restored. Each is outfitted as an example of its type, one being converted into a typical blacksmith shop. That one, originally home to the Rowe-Maddox family, ironically held a story that well might have involved the sheriff and the old jail had matters taken a slightly different course. In 1878, the women of the house were alone while their men folk went to help build a church. Two strangers stopped in and commandeered the bedroom for the night. Terrified, the women stayed on guard in the kitchen, armed only with an axe and a hoe. The strangers packed up and left before the men of the family returned with disturbing news. Two members of the Sam Bass gang had been spotted in the vicinity. Could these have been their uninvited visitors?

Through the years, more and more artifacts have been acquired, such as a grain crib and a ladies' mounting platform, which Mr. Bellamy said they might incorporate as a stile for crossing the WPA-built stone wall. A stone house has also been dismantled and will be reconstructed on the grounds. Evidence suggests that it may predate the oldest known house in the area. Mr. Bellamy says the additions have kept the Association busy, but the most pressing project at this time is to complete a climate controlled area for preserving old photographs and documents.

Meanwhile, hard attitudes of the past have relaxed. After all, by 1918 even Charles Goodnight gave up his guns to make a silent movie called *Old Texas,* in which he filmed his Kiowa friends staging a buffalo hunt.

A visit to the old jail and pioneer complex will give you a true picture of frontier life. Find it a block south of the courthouse in Palo Pinto, which is on U.S. 180. For information about visiting times or tours, contact: Palo Pinto County Pioneer Museum, 5th & Elm Street, Palo Pinto, TX 76484. (940) 659-2555. Or Chamber of Commerce, P.O. Box 1408, Mineral Wells, TX 76068. (940) 325-2557 or visit their website at: www.mineralwellstx.com

*Palo Pinto County Jail current appearance.*

*The first Frio County Jail at abandoned Frio Town.*
*Photograph by Dr. Robert Gorhum.*

# Pearsall
# Frio County Jails
## (1872 and 1884-1967)
### Frio Pioneer Jail Museum

Pearsall and Frio Town make their own "tale of two cities." Situated at the Frio River crossing, Frio Town seemed like a perfect spot, and as county seat, it built a two-story jail in 1872, the top floor of which served as a jury room. Unfortunately, records report that in as little as three years, the building couldn't "retain prisoners," and the county couldn't afford to hire guards or make repairs. Sheriff W.S. Hiller had to take dangerous felons to neighboring Medina County for safekeeping. Yet at some point that jail had held Jesse and Frank James and, according to tradition, Sam Bass too.

Then on July 4, 1881, the first passenger train pulled into what is now Pearsall with the International Great Northern Railroad selling lots for this new town, which happened to be named after a railroad official. The tracks missed Frio Town by about fifteen miles, so most businesses moved to Pearsall, and in 1883, citizens voted to move the county seat there as well.

Until they got a new county jail built, Sheriff W.C. Daugherty had to take prisoners from the Frio Town Jail to the Bexar County Jail. Builders of the new lockup evidently aimed to remedy past flaws. They contracted the Pauly Jail Company, which had by this time made escapes a thing of the past—almost. Since part of the building plan was to keep the sheriff or a jailer on the premises by providing a home for his family, the county wouldn't have to hire extra guards or even a cook. Also, since a jail needed to be close to the courthouse in the heart of town, it needed to be handsome, as this one certainly is.

The only jail part of the bottom floor was the sheriff's office, where he booked prisoners, and the stairway up to the cells. You can still see the opening in the wall through which food trays were passed. In the main cell block, surrounded by a runaround, each cell could hold four men. Installed later were two more cells, separated from the main area. These were for women, juveniles, and "occasionally for maniacs," as the book *Historic Frio County* states. During Prohibition, however, one of the cells stored bootleg liquor. The book also reports that prominent citizens were held there until they were able to make bond.

Every jailer will attest to the obsession of certain prisoners to find a way out. Some methods take more effort than the inmate ever expended on honest work, and one of these efforts in the Pearsall Jail is evident forever. The metal door into the main cell block has the usual "squint." This barred, eye level enclosure protrudes into a cellblock door so a jailer can safely put his head into it and look around to avoid an ambush. One prisoner, who must have been quite skinny, sawed through several thick bars in the squint and pried aside others. Then greasing his body, he wriggled through the opening and somehow got outside. He was never seen again, but I'd bet he carried scars to his grave.

Dora Jo Smith Carter, daughter of Sheriff Warren Smith, remembers another bad incident when her family lived in the jail during her father's tenure, 1937-1949. Prisoners started a fire, but luckily firemen put it out before it spread to the lower floor. Unfortunately, water flooding the downstairs made quite a mess.

Depression years notwithstanding, most of Dora's memories of growing up in the jail were pleasant: lots of company and the big meals her mother cooked for them and the prisoners; the thick masonry walls keeping the house cooler than most houses; the shade of a huge grape arbor where they had church picnics and birthday parties; the menagerie of animals her father kept; a big yard well-kept by jail trustees; and the fact that she was the only kid in town whose bedroom (converted from the lobby) had bars on the windows.

Sheriff Smith had been in law enforcement most of his adult life, starting as a Texas Ranger. After leaving the Rangers, Smith was a personal body guard to a wealthy man in Fort Worth. He served at the Huntsville State Penitentiary and was there during a massive riot in 1934. Ready for a more peaceful life, Smith took a position as deputy sheriff in Pearsall, but when the sheriff died in office, he was selected to take the reins of leadership and continued to do so for the next dozen years.

Those are the years Dora most remembers, even though she didn't always understand events fully, such as a headline that read, "Sheriff Smith Captures Texas Public Enemy Number One Without Firing a Shot!" She does know that he was well-respected, especially by Mexican-Americans, both because of his fair treatment and because he spoke fluent Spanish. Many a time local citizens helped Smith by reporting situations that could have led to more trouble. After his tenure as sheriff ended, he "retired" to ranching.

The building was retired, too, in 1967, when a new jail was built. In 1976 the old jail became the Frio Pioneer Jail Museum. Dignitaries at the dedication ceremony included Representative Henry Gonzalez and Frio County's own woman sheriff, Ollie Taylor. When the current president of the Frio County Historical Society, Dr. Robert Gorhum, led us through the building, it had recently celebrated the town's annual Pioneer Days celebration and showed evidence that a large crowd had been on hand at the jail and the adjacent Firemen's Park.

Exhibits are arranged in glass cases or mounted on the wall, or as room arrangements creatively barricaded, not with the usual ropes, but by railings from the historic courthouse. A large array of photographs and artifacts trace the county's history, including tributes to that other county seat that turned into the ghost of Frio Town.

The jail is the oldest building in town, but the exterior is as pretty as if it had been built yesterday. It still even has its windmill and well. Look for it at Cedar and Medina Streets. For information about visiting times or tours, contact: Frio Pioneer Jail Museum Association, c/o Dr. Robert J. Gorhum, D.D.S., 310 S. Oak St., Pearsall, TX 78061. (830) 334-4181; or Chamber of Commerce: (830) 334-9414 or visit their website at: www.pearsalltexas.com/history.htm

*Frio County Jail current appearance.*

*The wolf hunt at Quanah. (l to r, standing) Lee Bivens, Capt. Bill McDonald, Jack Abernathy, Maj. S.B. Young, Capt. Burk Burnett, Col. Theodore Roosevelt, L.M. Gillis. (sitting) two U.S. soldiers unidentified, R.L. More, Guy Waggoner, Chief Quanah Parker (kneeling), Cecil Lyons, Dr. Lambert, and D.P. Taylor.*
*Photo courtesy of the Hardeman County Historical Society.*

# Quanah
# Hardeman County Jail
## (1891-1973)
## Hardeman County Historical Museum

The town of Quanah is named for the last great Comanche war chief, Quanah Parker. He gave the town his blessing: "May the Great Spirit smile on your little town. . . . May peace and contentment be with you and your children forever." Just as the chief made a full transition from warpath to friendliness in the twentieth century, the town has transitioned from a wild past to law and order in the twenty-first.

Quanah's mother, Cynthia Ann Parker, at the age of nine, was kidnapped and sold to the Comanches, but she grew up and became wife to the chief and mother to Quanah and his brother and sister. A force of Texas Rangers raided her tribe's camp while the braves were away hunting. The Rangers killed many, and "saved" Cynthia Ann at the sight of her blue eyes, delivering her and her three-year-old daughter, Prairie Flower, to her original family. Prairie Flower languished and died, and by 1871, Cynthia Ann also died in grief over the loss of her husband and children.

Meanwhile, Quanah, having adopted the name "Parker" in her honor, had lost his whole family, too. By 1867 he was a leader of his tribe. When U.S. government officials convinced other Indians to give up their homelands and move to reservations in Oklahoma, Quanah Parker and his band kept fighting. A federation of Comanches, Kiowas, Chyennes, and Arapahos joined together to fight the U.S. Army under the leadership of Quanah Parker, but they were no match for the Americans' greatly superior weapons.

The U.S. Army set out to defeat the remaining hostiles by destroying their horses, homes, food, and weapons. It worked. Quanah Parker recognized that further resistance would lead to the annihilation of his people, so he adapted and eventually surrendered in 1875. On the reservation, he learned English, business practices, and negotiation skills. He became certified as a judge on one of the Courts of Indian Offenses to settle disputes within the reservation. Several times he traveled to Washington D.C. to represent the Indians, in the process winning many influential friends. A photo of a wolf hunt shows him with a few of these friends near the town of Quanah.

After a few years on the reservation living in teepees, Quanah, along with his wives and children, received the gift of a large white house from his friend, cattle baron Burk Burnett, who called it the "Comanche White House." It remains in good condition at Cache, Oklahoma. Quanah Parker was also proud of the town in Texas named after him and visited it many times. He died in 1911, and a monument to him stands on the courthouse square. His abilities to adapt and to help others adjust saved countless lives on both sides of the conflict.

Having Indians on reservations did not solve all the white man's problems, however. Desperadoes who had accumulated in and around the panhandle were used to doing as they pleased and they didn't cotton to the newer settlers' pleas for law and order. It was in this atmosphere that Bill and Rhoda McDonald moved to Hardeman County sometime after 1883. He accepted the job of deputy sheriff, thus beginning his legend as a lawman who was never arrogant or boastful.

People soon started to repeat a saying that "he would charge hell with a bucket of water." No doubt he furnished plenty of business for the jail at

Quanah. Before long he became a Deputy U.S. Marshal, and by 1891 he was appointed Captain of Company B, Frontier Battalion of the Texas Rangers.

In 1893, he was involved in the most exciting gun battle that ever happened in Quanah. Sheriff John Mathews from the nearby town of Childress had become angry at Captain McDonald and spread the word that he was going over to Quanah and kill McDonald. The *Quanah Tribune-Chief's* centennial edition reported that Mathews came to Quanah, "accompanied by a group of henchmen and sight-seers." When McDonald didn't materialize for a showdown, Mathews and his followers decided to go back home. But just before the train arrived, McDonald appeared and asked Mathews of his intentions.

The Hardeman County Sheriff Dick Coffer managed to get between the two men as Mathews drew his pistol and fired over Coffer's shoulder. The bullet went through McDonald's coat collar while he moved to the side in an effort to miss Coffer as he shot at Mathews. Two slugs hit Mathews in the left side of his chest but were stopped by a bullet-proof device. Mathews shot McDonald, but the wound didn't stop the enraged Texas Ranger, and McDonald changed his aim to get around Mathews' shield. This time it dropped Mathews, but some of his followers opened fire on McDonald. McDonald, injured to the point he couldn't use his right hand, proceeded to cock the gun with his teeth. The followers had seen enough and ran off.

Mathews was put on the train and taken back home but died after a few days.

McDonald, shot four times, recovered and continued going after bad guys until 1918 when he died. His tombstone in Quanah Memorial Park Cemetery sums up his philosophy in his own words: "No man in the wrong can stand up against a man in the right who keeps on a-coming."

Many of those McDonald captured spent at least some time in the old jail, and violent crime had lessened through the years. The last sheriff who housed his family there, which included his ten children, was Chester Ingram. Former Sheriff Ingram became city mayor, but plans to retire when his son, who grew up in the jail, takes office as County Judge. Ingram spent seven years as a deputy and twenty-eight as the county sheriff. He told of two jail breaks that occurred while he was sheriff.

One prisoner had been in jail for a couple of weeks while officers continued to look for his partner in crime who was still on the loose. One

Sunday while the sheriff and his family were gone, the elusive partner broke into the jail, got the keys, and released his buddy, thoughtfully locking all the other prisoners back in. The two left the jail, but they didn't get far. One was apprehended in Oklahoma and the other in Louisiana.

The other jailbreak also occurred on a Sunday. A visitor had slipped one of the prisoners a saw blade, so he sawed out just enough to wriggle through. Then somehow the convict picked the lock to get out through the main jail door and escaped. The rest of the prisoners were hollering when Ingram came back, so he put out a call immediately. The prisoner was found cooling off in a bar in Oklahoma.

The jail closed in 1973 when a newer facility was built. Since then, the Hardeman County Historical Society has turned the lower floor into a museum, but plans to keep the cells as they were. The group also operates the Quanah Acme & Pacific Railway Depot Museum next to the Old Jail, so visitors can see both in one trip.

The old jail is located at 105 Green Street between 1st & 2nd Street, back to back with the restored Depot on Mercer St. For information about visiting times or tours, contact: Hardeman County Museum, 105 Green Street, Quanah, TX 79252-4039. (940) 663-5932 or the Chamber of Commerce (940) 663-2222.

*Old Jail with Depot Museum behind it. Gina Daugherty photographer.*

*The Bexar County Jail circa 1940s. Courtesy of Alamo City Hotels.*

## San Antonio
# Bexar County Jail
## (1878-1962)
## Comfort Inn Alamo River Walk

Who says cities have to knock down their old buildings to keep up with progress? San Antonio is famous for, not only saving its historical properties, but capitalizing on them, and in 2005 it demonstrated again how to adapt to a changing world while honoring the past. The 1878 Bexar County Jail, a mere three blocks from the renowned River Walk, instead of being razed, became a hotel.

Comparatively, an 1878 building is new-kid-on-the-block to the area where it's situated, the Main Plaza and Military Plaza, which were named in honor of the King of Spain almost two centuries earlier. San Fernando de Bexar, as San Antonio was named first, was the first chartered civilian settlement in Texas, but conflict with Apaches and Comanches made it difficult to attract a population. Notes at the hotel state that in 1749, "Spaniards made peace with the Apaches by burying a live horse with a tomahawk, a lance, and six arrows in the Plaza." Whether or not this worked, the documents didn't say, but other sources report no noticeable growth in the economy and population at that time.

During the Texas Revolution, the fate of the Alamo rallied Texians to make the Republic of Texas a reality. Unfortunately, when Texas became a state in the United States, first joined, then seceded, then readmitted, its wild west status attracted more than its share of outlaws, and San Antonio was a major travel route.

No wonder the citizens built the large Bexar County Jail in 1878, originally two stories high. They employed famous architect Alfred Giles to design the building. Construction of the historic courthouse didn't come until the 1890s.

Over the years, floors were added to the jail, once in 1911 and again in 1926, until it reached its present five story height. Each of those stories has extra high ceilings, as the tall windows dictate. Since the street the building is located on is named "Cameron," the Spanish word for "shrimp," prisoners dubbed it "the Shrimp Hotel."

In 1921, convicted murderer Clemente Apolinar had the distinction of being the last person hanged in the old Bexar County Jail. He not only killed a teenage boy, but also gouged out the boy's eyes to carry around in his pocket. Only a couple of years after the hanging, Texas discontinued that method of execution, as well as each county taking care of its own. Co-authors James Marquart, Sheldon Ekland-Olson, and Jonathan Sorensen, in their book *The Rope, The Chair, and the Needle: Capital Punishment in Texas, 1923-1990* stated that the rope used for Bexar County's last execution was purchased by former Sheriff John W. Tobin. Later it was loaned to the sheriff of Brewster County for a hanging and then returned afterward to Bexar County Sheriff James Stevens. Once hanging went out, Bexar County used it as a tow rope.

In 1962 when a new jail was built, the old jail was vacated. Years later Bexar County Jail, Ltd., bought and renovated it to use for archival storage.

Late in 1983 the facade donation was made to the San Antonio Conservation Society, which accepts the "facade easements" of historic structures as a means of insuring their preservation. The organization then posts the availability of the property, possibly for adaptive use. (See section on "Jails Waiting" to see how this worked for other cities, too. Most are not open to the public as this one is.)

At last in 2002, Alamo City Hotels by Serene Lodging, Inc., bought the building and transformed it into a Comfort Inn. This conversion took three years, but the results are superb. The tall ceilings and windows and the plush furnishings give each room a rich, historic look, but thank goodness, not the original historic look the jail had for its first 127 years. Some of the rooms have kept the bars on their windows, oddly right-looking with the elegant draperies, but eighty-eight sets of window bars, each weighing over 400 pounds, had to be cut out.

Likewise, a thirteen-step steel stairway leading to the hanging room on the third floor had to be removed. To name a few of the challenges, gallows openings on the second and third floors, through which the body could drop to the first floor, had to be filled in. But developers said the most daunting task was finding ways to accommodate twenty-first century technology.

San Antonio not only "Remembers the Alamo!" but also its other historic treasures, and it has made tourism big business. Now it even gives us a way to go to jail and like it.

For information about visiting times or tours, contact: Comfort Inn Alamo River walk, 120 Cameron St. San Antonio, TX 78205. (210) 281-1400 or (800) 223-4990 or visit their website at: www.AlamoCityHotels.com or www.ComfortInnSanAntonio.com

*Bexar County Jail now the Comfort Inn, Alamo River Walk.*

*El Paso County Jail. Courtesy of the San Elizario Genealogy and Historical Society.*

# San Elizario
# El Paso County Jail
## (1850-1940s)
### Jail Museum on Historic District Tour

The oldest still viable jail building I found incorporates adobe bricks from an even older wall, that of a defensive Spanish *presidio*. The usual meaning of this word is "fortress or garrison of soldiers," and indeed this town was that. But *Velázquez Spanish and English Dictionary* adds another definition: "a place for punishing criminals by hard labor." Fitting for a jail.

In 1850, when El Paso County was created, San Elizario was its largest and most prosperous town, a major stop on the Butterfield Overland Stage route through the mountain pass carved by the Rio Grande. Therefore, it was selected as the county seat. Even if every citizen had been law-abiding, imagine the hoards of "forty-niner" fortune seekers on their way to the California gold rush—it no doubt needed a jail.

The adobe building San Elizarians started with to make a jail-courthouse is thought to have been a residence during the Mexican period, which could date it as early as the 1820s. A prefabricated riveted strap-iron cage was installed with two cells designed to hold six prisoners. The rest of the 1,200 square foot building was then completed around it, adobe bricks with a roof supported by cottonwood logs or *vigas*.

The most often-told story names this as "the only jail Billy the Kid broke into." In 1876 or 1877 a friend of Billy named Segura had been arrested and jailed in San Elizario. Segura was in danger of being lynched, and as soon as Billy heard about it, he rode out of New Mexico and arrived at the jail in the middle of the night. Legend states that Billy woke the guards as he called from outside the door, claiming to be a Texas Ranger with prisoners. One guard opened the door and met the muzzle of Billy's .44 revolver. Billy made the guards unlock Segura's cell and unshackle him from the post he was chained to. The Kid forced the two guards to trade places with Segura and then he threw away the key. He and Segura crossed the Rio Grande River into Mexico.

Segura kept going, but Billy returned to New Mexico where he was engaged in the Lincoln County War. By the time Sheriff Pat Garrett gunned him down, Billy the Kid had gunned down more men than the number of years he'd lived.

Although there is no documentation to prove the tale about the San Elizario jail break, it is corroborated in Pat Garrett's *Authentic Life of Billy the Kid* (published in 1882 after the Kid was dead), supposedly quoting the written record of a member of Garrett's posse.

But wait a minute! Who really started the story? That was the question a researcher named Skip Clark asked. Currently on the board for "San Eli's" Mission Trail Association, Clark has long been involved in the archeology and effort to restore the area's buildings, including the jail. "It was serendipity," Clark says that led him to make the William Bonney (aka Billy the Kid) legend the subject of his master's thesis.

Clark made some excellent points while verifying the San Elizario Jail break. Younger generations remembered hearing the story from Spanish-speaking local residents, who lived there about the time the incident would have happened. Does it make sense they might have waited half a dozen years, and then read a book about it, written in English? Clark suggests that, since Garrett was working as a customs official in El Paso, he might well have heard the story in Spanish (which he understood well) about the time he started writing his book.

At any rate, these were troubled times when jail records were spotty at best, and in 1877, officials had something bigger to think about than Billy the Kid. The gory and brutal Salt War undoubtedly furnished plenty of business for the jail, as well as for the local undertaker. For generations, salt deposits about a hundred miles east of town had been free for the taking. Contention arose when former county judge Charles Howard laid claim to the area and shot a man over it. Mob violence ensued, and a company of Texas Rangers came in and took Howard under their protection. The mob murdered Howard and some of the Rangers before order was regained. It is said this was the only time Texas Rangers were defeated. As a result, Fort Bliss, abandoned at the beginning of the Civil War, was re-garrisoned.

Another war of the political kind arose when the county seat was switched back and forth between Ysleta and San Elizario twice, but in 1883, the prized position landed in El Paso, which had become a boom town since railroad lines converged through the settlement. The little jail at San Elizario continued to be used through the 1940s for short-term offenders. In fact, Skip Clark says law officers even used it in the 1970s, when necessary, as a holding tank.

Museum Director Chito Parra related a story from another resident. The man says that lawmen would lock prisoners in the iron cages but leave the outer door open so they could call to passersby when they needed something. Parra commented, "Imagine walking past the deserted old jail and hearing a call, 'Can anybody hear me?' from the dark interior."

Clark says eventually jail reforms prohibited its use for prisoners, but somebody used the building for a little grocery store for a while. After the building fell into disuse, it also fell into disrepair. By the new millennium it became clear that something had to be done to save this structure that was on the National Register of Historic Places. In 2003 the county offered the Texas Historical Commission a plan for preserving the jail. The plan was approved, and the THC grant was matched by El Paso County. This was only the beginning.

The traditional mud plaster coating had not been maintained to protect the adobe bricks. To make matters worse, newer concrete footings didn't allow the adobe "to breathe." Consequently, just as other masonry walls do in the "rising damp" of retained moisture, these ancient walls were disintegrating. The contractors, Wright and Dalbin, came up with more permanent and strengthening coatings while making the walls look as they did in 1850.

The old jail is part of the San Elizario Historic District Tour.

For information about visiting times or tours, contact: San Elizario Genealogy and Historical Society, P.O. Box 1090, San Elizario, TX 79849. (915) 851-1682 or visit their website at: www.rootsweb.com/~txseghs

*El Paso County Jail. Photo by Barclay Gibson.*

*1873 Hays County's First Jail.*

## San Marcos
# First Hays County Jail
## (1873-1885)
## Calaboose African American
## History Museum

To look at San Marcos's first jail, a small, one-story brick house, you wouldn't think it could have held more than two or three bad guys at a time. But appearances hid a gruesome secret. Its ten-by-eighteen-foot underground dungeon sometimes held as many as twenty prisoners. It took a lawyer's imprisonment and tragedy to bring the miserable conditions to public attention. The jail was built in 1873 during the Reconstruction period, which didn't end in Texas until the following year.

Sheriff Zachariah (Zack) Pierpoint Bugg was the county's first sheriff, and before a jail was constructed he had to take dangerous prisoners to the Travis County Jail in Austin for safe keeping. Ordinary prisoners were customarily ironed and kept by citizens. Hays County Police Court Records of the times shows that citizens were paid $95 for boarding, while the sheriff was paid $50 "for all services."

One pre-jail historical account barely mentions a stagecoach robbery shortly after the "War of Secession." It happened in Hays County between the stagecoach's destination points of Dallas and San Antonio. Since an unnamed robber and sheriff were both mentioned, we must assume that it was Sheriff Zack Bugg who dealt with it. Bugg was apparently well respected, and modern residents are proud of the fact that he was the great-great grandfather of movie actor Robert Redford.

By 1873, Hays County received permission from the State Legislature to build a jail. Underneath the present concrete floor lies a track for three separate cells that shared a common door, but the cells are now gone. The dungeon was long ago filled in, but drilling points show where the dimensions were verified. Two fireplaces original to the building were removed at some point.

Thanks to the San Marcos newspaper of the time, the *West Texas Free Press*, copies of which are on file at the museum, more detailed accounts began about that time. The notorious Belle Starr spent time in this jail. Then in June 1874, a jail break took place in which three prisoners hiding in the privy attacked the jailer and threw him into one of the cells. Twelve prisoners escaped, and as the reporter wrote: "Great excitement prevailed . . . there was an instant 'mounting in hot haste the steed,' six-shooters in hand . . . as glimpses of the pursuers and pursued were had scudding across the corn-fields . . ." All were recaptured, except the two charged with murder! However, the article ends on a note of confidence, "The two . . . will hardly permanently make good their escape." Were they caught? We'll never know.

It was during Sheriff Barber's tenure that the *Free Press* published a series of articles regarding the deplorable conditions in the jail dungeon due to overcrowding. Lawyer Paul Hudson, charged with forgery, wrote letters to the county judge and commissioners (also an alleged letter to Sheriff Barber) pleading for lawful, humane treatment for detainees in the dungeon, some of whom hadn't even been proven guilty. Mr. Hudson cited that the place was alive with vermin, had no ventilation even in the stifling heat, and that prisoners, so crowded they couldn't lie down without overlapping each other, were forced to live as "filthy as hogs." Being ironed and kept outside would have been preferable. He further stated the irony that two prisoners incarcerated for murder had been sent to the comparative comfort of a jail in a neighboring county, because of the danger of keeping them in such a situation.

As if that were not sad enough, on February 12, 1884, Mr. Hudson also wrote one suicide letter each to his wife, to his mother, and to his "companions in misery" in the jail. Then he crushed some glass and drank it in a carbolic acid cocktail. After several hours, he died.

But the idea did not die with him. The *Free Press* published the letters and all subsequent reactions to them from February 12 to March 20, along with such editorial comments as: "We feel sure none of our commissioners would leave a horse or dog in such a place as our jail, on a hot summer night." The *Bastrop Advertiser* too reported the San Marcos Jail to be so "utterly unfit to live in without injury to health that prisoners suicide rather than live in it."

# Second Hays County Jail (1885- ?)

Public condemnation of the overcrowding, with its attendant problems, led the county to construct Jail #2 in 1885. It stands on the same block with Jail #1, and appears to have been a magnificent structure, two stories tall, built of stone. It remains at this writing as a fitting home for a family of turkey buzzards, which have nested there for four generations, states Johnnie Armstead, founder, curator, and board president of the museum.

Even after Jail #2 was built, however, Jail #1 did not close down, but was used for black prisoners. It also held the mentally ill until they could be transferred to Austin. It took on a patriotic cause during World War II when the county added a wooden extension to serve as a USO (United Service Organizations, Inc., a voluntary civilian social service agency for people in the armed forces) for black servicemen stationed at Air Corps Navigation School (later called Camp Gary). After that, the building came into use for a recreation center and meeting place.

Since 1997, Jail #1 has been in use as the Calaboose African American History Museum. A board of trustees, under the leadership of Mrs. Armstead, has turned it into an attractive and comprehensive display that highlights African American heritage in San Marcos. The organization fosters various programs throughout the year. Besides the Calaboose, which is in good condition, three other buildings in the area (Jail #2, a large church, and the home of an influential blacksmith) are slated for renovation at a cost of five million dollars.

The blacksmith, a black man named Ulyssis Cephas, prevented much grief as a "go-between" for the black community with the Ku Klux Klan. On one occasion, members of the KKK told Cephas that a certain young black youth had better leave town for a while until things cooled off after the young man was said to have looked at a white woman a little too long. This probably saved the kid's life. Such intervention, unfortunately, did not always happen.

In recent years, an anonymous donor brought in a KKK uniform, formerly owned by one of his deceased forebears, to add to the museum's display. Another property was recently returned, a small wooden building that had stood originally on the same grounds with the Calaboose. It had for years represented a jail in a "pioneer village" at the theme park at Aquarena Springs, also in San Marcos. Since Aquarena has become a research and conservation facility owned by Texas State University instead of a theme park, the "jail" has come back home. However, Mrs. Armstead says she has so far not found any documentation that it was used to hold prisoners.

Hays County sold the property to San Marcos in 1885, and the complex is currently part of the City Parks and Recreation facilities. The Calaboose was featured in the Texas Historical Commission publication *Texas in World War II* (2005).

Mrs. Armstead visits schools and other groups with her "Traveling Trunk" demonstrations. For information about visiting times, tours, and special events, contact: Calaboose African American History Museum, 200 Martin Luther King Drive, San Marcos, TX 78666. (512) 353-0124 e-mail them at: calaboose@centurytel.net

*Resident buzzard on 1885 second jail. Courtesy of the Calaboose Museum.*

*Donated relic, Ku Klux Klan robe and hood found in the museum.*

# Silverton
# Briscoe County Jail
## (1894-1972)
## Old Jail Museum

Not prairie fires, grasshopper swarms, or cyclones can defeat Silverton. Even after a killer tornado in 1957, the town rebuilt, and with Lake Mackenzie nearby as an attraction, and the fact that there's only one other town in Briscoe County, it's likely to continue. The little stone jail standing next to the main highway symbolizes that spirit.

The county was proudly named after Andrew Briscoe, who fought in the War for Texas Independence during both the Battle of Concepcion and the Battle of San Jacinto. Briscoe eventually became the Chief Justice of Harris County. A latter-day Thomas Briscoe who settled in the area started the fledgling town's first newspaper, the *Silverton Light*.

The jail locked up its first inmate at the opening ceremony in 1894—Sheriff Miner Crawford—for fun. The respect people held for him was no laughing matter, however, and he helped bring order to a lawless territory. His first official duty was to arrest a couple of New Mexico horse thieves who thought they could live free in Texas. Years later citizens even brought Sheriff Crawford back to serve two more separate terms, ending in 1922. In his last term, Crawford and two deputies had a shootout with some moon shiners and captured their still in the encounter.

Silverton was very much an Old West town, with mail delivered by stagecoach up until 1928 when, at last, the railroad reached it. Early sheriffs' families rented the lower floor as a residence, so it is displayed in that fashion today. It closed briefly as a jail during World War I and was used by the Red Cross.

The old jail on the square is on Highway 86, and caretaker, Jerry Baker, is often on hand to show it to visitors. For information about visiting times or tours, contact: County Offices, (806) 823-2132 or visit the Chamber of Commerce website at: www.silvertontexas.com

*Briscoe County Jail current appearance. Ernest Upton photographer.*

*A photograph detailing the interior of the Briscoe County Jail.*

*Wharton County Jail circa 1888. Courtesy of the Wharton County Historical Museum.*

## Wharton
# Wharton County Jail
## (1888-1938)
## 20th Century Technology Museum

Other cities may demolish their old jails, but Wharton has recycled all seven: the latest (built in 1996) is still in use; two (dating 1854 and 1936) are residences; two small holding jails (dates unknown) are still standing; one former plantation jail (date unknown) is being restored; and the 1888 jail now houses the 20th Century Technology Museum. Talk about adaptive uses—Wharton, we salute you!

Let's focus on the latter two as opposite ends of the county's rich history. In 1823, during Mexico's Anglo-American colonization of Texas territory, thirty-one of Stephen F. Austin's "Old Three Hundred" were granted titles to land in what is now Wharton County. Coming mostly from southern states, these settlers recreated their new life in Texas like it had been in the Old South. Many of the men eventually fought in the Texas Revolution. By the time of the Civil War, Wharton County had the largest plantation and sugar mill in Texas, but the thriving economy and way of life collapsed during and after the war, while the ranks of the Ku Klux Klan swelled.

Prior to the Civil War there had been a county jail, but plantation owners apparently cooperated to build their own. Abandoned and forgotten after the plantations broke up, these buildings disappeared under a tangle of undergrowth.

Fast-forwarding to the present, Art Schulze, who formerly subcontracted engineering services for NASA and now designs electronic healthcare devices, bought land just out of town. When Schulze began to clear the property in 1999, he discovered a small brick building, filled with litter, its roof caved in, and trees crowding the walls. Hand-hewn logs in the rafters and door frame alerted Schulze to its historical value. Old timers remembered at least one similar building having collapsed from neglect. Some people said they had grown up being told this was an old jail, while others told of different purposes it had served. Perhaps the most convincing statement came from an elderly patient of Schulze's physician son. The man attested to having been locked in that jail before. At any rate, the old building, possibly a plantation jail dating back to the 1850s, is now cleaned up, re-roofed, and secured with hope for a future.

The antebellum Wharton County Jail, which records state was built in 1854, continued to operate until the second county jail came along. It was purchased and turned into a home, as it remains to this day. The 1888, two-story brick building was done in High Victorian, Italianate style, a noble structure, befitting one of the town's greatest law enforcement heroes.

Not all gun-toting sheriffs held their shootouts at high noon like in western movies. One day in 1894, Wharton County Sheriff Hamilton B. Dickson joined Sheriff J.L. Townsend of the next county to track a fugitive who had escaped from jail, killing a constable in the process. Sheriff Dickson came up on the fugitive, who shot and murdered the escapee at close range. Dickson in turn was killed by a member of the posse. For Dickson's funeral, chartered trains brought people from distant places to pay their respects. Today the town has a monument to him.

The jail stayed in operation for over forty years before it was retired from service. The next jail, built in 1938, happens to sit right next door to its predecessor, and it also had a well-known sheriff, famous in an entirely different way. Sheriff Tom "Buckshot" Lane was elected constable for eight years and sheriff for the next twelve, proving his popularity in the local community. Radio station KULP in El Campo gave him a regular morning program, in which he would occasionally call the name of someone with an arrest warrant, telling him, "Don't make me come after you." As often as not, those so summoned gave themselves up. They knew his reputation for fearlessness and persistence. In one shootout, his car ended up with fifty-two bullet holes. It was his opponent who, as Buckshot said, "never got over it."

Not only his shoot-'em-up style endeared him to the public though. His honesty was legendary, and he was always ready to take on new law-enforcement skills. He first learned fingerprinting. He then taught himself to fly a plane. Because there was no money in the county coffers to buy him an aircraft, he asked his constituents to donate a dollar each for the cause. He ended up with more than enough money, and painted each donor's name on the "People's Airplane," or the "Stinson Station Wagon," as one *New York Times* reporter called it in 1949. *Life* magazine also ran an article about Buckshot in 1950. People kept writing about him even after he passed away.

Meanwhile, the county had been using the 1888 jailhouse for various offices until the building was purchased by David Bucek, a restoration architect with Stern and Bucek. He has practiced his trade on quite a bit of the historic building since. The jail's steel cells are long gone from the second floor, but the first floor is restored, including the beautiful staircase and terrazzo floors. Two thousand feet of this floor has been transformed into the recently opened 20th Century Technology Museum.

Art Schulze, the man who unearthed the old plantation jail, happens to be "overseer" of the museum project. Along with his wife Sharon, and owner Bucek, Schulze has put together this unique museum. The answer to the frequently asked question shows up on the website: "While [technology] may seem too recent a subject for a historical museum, with the rapid pace of technological change, items from the first half of the 20th century are truly 'museum pieces' at this point. Technology from the latter half of the century may not seem so antiquated, but items from this period help to show how the earlier items relate to current technology."

As reporter Benjamin Sharp of the *Wharton Journal-Spectator* pointed out in one article, "It's eye-opening to see how technology has advanced . . . chronicling technological growth in several fields: communication, household devices, computation instrumentation, and aviation."

And what of the jail section? Schulze says he would love to see the museum expanded to the entire building. While the upstairs still needs renovation, and the cells are gone, the history and mystery still wait: a photo of the last hanging, done in about 1914, is on file and part of a very old rope hangs in one of the rooms. "Besides," Schulze adds, "the location is excellent, and the scenery overlooking the river is spectacular from the second floor."

For information about visiting times or tours, contact: 20th Century Technology Museum, 231 S. Fulton, Wharton, TX 77488. (979) 282-8810 or visit their website at: www.20thcenturytech.com

*Wharton County Jail current appearance.*
*Courtesy of the 20th Century Technology Museum.*

# JAILS WAITING
## Not open to the Public at this Time

*Bee County Jail current appearance.*

## Beeville
# Bee County Jail
## (1874)
### near courthouse square

The board-and-batten structure standing near the present Beeville Courthouse may not look impressive, but think again. This is one of the best surviving examples of a typical early jail, and it served as the county's only lockup for nineteen years. The single iron-shuttered window and two barred windows furnished the only air-conditioning. In the *Bee Picayune's* centennial edition, long-time resident Mac Powell wrote about his memory of it: "How could a man live for one night . . . in that den?" John Hester, another long-time resident, said it was moved away from the square because of its humble appearance for quite some time. I was glad to see it's back near the courthouse once more.

*Burnet County Jail current appearance.*

# Burnet
# Burnet County Jail
## (1884)
### corner of Washington and Pierce Streets

Burnet's last downtown gunfight took place in 1911, and no town needed a jail more. Sheriff Wallace Riddell, who housed his family there, set the tone for a more law-abiding atmosphere. He held office from 1939 to 1978, the longest tenure of any sheriff in America. Darrell Debo, of the Burnet Historical Board, says Riddell never made any special election efforts to keep his office. His way of life was all the campaigning he needed. A negotiator before such a specialty was given a name, he never wore a gun and was able to defuse volatile situations. Debo recalls at least one incident involving minors in which Riddell "talked the boys out of trouble" and returned them to their parents instead of locking them in jail. A statue of Debo stands on the courthouse grounds.

The old jail is currently a probation office.

*Leon County Jails on courthouse square current appearance.*

## Centerville
# Leon County Jails
## (1887, 1913, 1974)
### on courthouse square

Towns often built their jails on the courthouse square to minimize the distance of escorting prisoners to court. Centerville has three closed jails on its square, and like most vintage buildings, all need some repairs. The Leon County Heritage Commission has its hands full. Restoration of the courthouse has to come first, and the group's president says work is underway.

Regarding the jails, the best known legend regards a prisoner who lived to tell of his own lynching in 1910. This prisoner, we'll call "Joe," along with his father and brother, had been tried for murder, but the jury was undecided. When Deputy Jeff St. Johns went up to the cells, Joe's father shot and wounded him. Joe and his father tried to escape, but an angry crowd chased them down, shooting the father. Joe and his badly injured father were recaptured and hauled back to jail. The mob strung up both from the rafters, but a Methodist preacher convinced the mob to cut them down. The officially reported cause of death for the father was gunshot wounds received while resisting arrest. The deputy recovered. Joe also recovered, and again faced trial. He got a life sentence but served only eight years.

*Hartley County Jail current appearance.*

# Channing
# Hartley County Jail
## (ca. 1900)

### near courthouse

I n 1891, Channing was the general headquarters of the 3,000,000-acre XIT Ranch. Channing became the county seat when XIT cowboys hauled the original frame courthouse there from the town of Hartley. The brick courthouse and jail came later. The town lost some of its population when the ranch was liquidated, and even more when major highways bypassed the town.

Leslie Kistner, a third generation mayor, gave us a tour of the now vacant jail. She also showed us a letter to Santa Claus, written by a group of former inmates while the hoosegow was still in business. They requested, "one box good quality hacksaw blades, a Big Sur water bed, and a joint of good grade weed."

# Dallas
# Dallas City Jail
## (1908)
## 705 Ross Ave.

The law firm of Robertson & Railsback has served its time in the old Dallas Jail ever since 1982. They've sold the historic building to another law firm, Miley & Brown, PC. The attorneys won preservation awards for the remodeling, while keeping the original solitary confinement cell in the basement. In 1908, the building started out as Dallas's second city jail, police station, and city court. Law officers had to march prisoners four blocks to the "Old Red Courthouse." After World War II, when a newer jail replaced it, various business used it. It locked up canines as a dog pound, then tools as a hardware store, and finally cheese as a warehouse. It sat vacant for a time before the law firm bought it.

While you can't visit it unless you need a lawyer, it is listed on the West End Association's walking tour (www.dallaswestend.org) that "includes the Old Jail and the Landmark Center." In 2004 Jeremy Leonard, chairman for the Association, purchased the Landmark Center located next-door, to remodel its office space and bottom floor restaurant, store, and pub. Originally a warehouse, it had already been turned into offices in 1979, 96% of which were occupied by the F.B.I. for years!

*Tarrant County Criminal Justice Building current appearance.*
*Courtesy of John Roberts, AIA, owner-operator of the history promoting website:*
*www.fortwortharchitecture.com*

# Fort Worth
# Tarrant County Criminal Justice Building
## (1918)
### 200 W. Belknap

When Fort Worth replaced its nineteenth century jail with this building, it provided cell space for county and federal prisoners, offices for the district attorney and sheriff, a ward for the criminally insane, and a hospital ward with an operating room. Exterior construction of granite, brick and terra cotta has changed very little. The original windows on the lower floors were wood and the upper floors had steel casement windows for security, deeply recessed with bars located behind them, so they were not visible from the street. In 1951 and again in 1970 remodeling projects dropped the ceilings, converted the old jail floors into office space, and installed fixed pane windows. It is now the Civil Courts Building in Fort Worth. The Investigation Department of the District Attorney's Office occupies part of the building, and the remainder is occupied by the County Probation Department.

Downtown Fort Worth has become a model for downtown revitalization, preserving many of its buildings constructed between 1880 and 1930, and class "A" downtown office occupancy is at about 98%. Working with Historic Fort Worth and Downtown Fort Worth, Inc., John Roberts, AIA Texas Registered Architect, operates a website showing pictures and descriptions of historical buildings to promote vintage architecture for adaptive uses: www.fortwortharchitecture.com

*Gillespie County Jail current appearance.*

# Fredericksburg
# Gillespie County Jail
# (1885)
## near courthouse square

Gillespie County's fourth jail sits empty, across the street from the modern Law Enforcement Building, and surrounded by a town full of historical architecture. The jail just before this one burned down, killing a prisoner indicted for murder. Such experience prompted city fathers to build a fireproof jail, which even had indoor plumbing at a time when that was rare. In her book *Old Homes and Buildings of Fredericksburg*, author Elise Kowert says this didn't mean inmates were pampered. The bathroom fixtures were "crude iron," and and there was only a single wood heater in the upstairs cell block. She also described the stone walls around the jail being topped with broken glass to make "escape over the walls painful." After the jail was replaced in 1939, the building became a home for various residents and was later used for storage.

*Williamson County Jail current appearance.*

# Georgetown
# Williamson County Jail
# (1888)

## Austin Avenue, three blocks north
## of the courthouse

The French Bastille style building was never meant to look inviting. But the old Williamson County Jail is quite the star for scary movie sets. Richard Miles, supervisor for retrial services, reported about half a dozen of them by 2001. Most recently, famed directors Quentin Tarantino and Robert Rodriguez filmed *Grind House* there. At this time, the jail is open for public tours only on special occasions, such as bi-annual Brown Santa fund raisers. Part of its first floor houses the county's Health District Office.

Linda Bunte, one of the first women officers hired to the sheriff's department, and others hope to see it eventually turned into a law enforcement museum. The point where late nineteenth century and newer sections join (when the jail was expanded) would provide an exhibit in itself of jail technology. The art on the jail's walls is some of the most elaborate I've seen. Ironically, the most serene of these paintings (though not well-done) was created by notorious serial killer Henry Lee Lucas. He left a mural on his cell wall of a sweet little house with a grazing deer.

*Mills County Jail current appearance.*

# Goldthwaite
# Mills County Jail
## (1888)
### on courthouse square

It may tell us something that Goldthwaite's founding fathers constructed the jail before any other county building, even before establishing a
county seat. Following what newspaper reporter Flora Bowles described as
"a fifteen-year war of violence and bloodshed . . . waged between rival
groups," it took Texas Rangers to restore order. Nevertheless, more shootouts made state-wide news even into the 1960s in this now peaceful little
town. An active Historical Society started a museum in the jail, but since
they needed more space for exhibits (always a good sign), and the old jail
needed too many repairs (not a good sign), they have moved to a building
down the street.

*Mason County Jail current appearance.*

# Mason
# Mason County Jail
## (1895)
### facing courthouse

The remnants of old Fort Mason on a hill overlooking the town once had an officer on its staff named Lt. Col. Robert E. Lee. If his spirit could see the two-story, brownstone jail today, he would surely approve. This jail has been showing prisoners the error of their ways for 112 years, and surprisingly, it continues to do so—these days while inmates wear petal-pink uniforms. Jail administrator Melvin Wickey showed us the original sheriff's living space which has yielded to technology and all the equipment it takes to keep a modern county coordinated.

Librarian Jane Hoerster says only one man was ever sentenced to death in Mason County. He killed Sheriff Alan Murray in 1929. Sheriff P.C. Baird became a local legend for his fearlessness and determination, and folks called him "Old Sleuth."

*Collin County Prison current appearance.*

## McKinney
# Collin County Prison
## (1880)
### 115 S. Kentucky Street

One of the best meals I ever ate was in jail—the Prison Bars & Grill, converted from the county's old jail. Unfortunately, it's closed now. As a jail it served ninety-nine years and locked up some of the worst criminals of its time: in the nineteenth century, Frank James, and in the twentieth, Ray Hamilton of the Bonnie and Clyde Gang and "Tex" Watson of the Manson gang. One of its lesser known guests had the bizarre habit of eating light bulbs. The only way Sheriff Tom Montgomery could keep illumination in the cell was to collect burned out bulbs to satisfy the inmate's appetite.

When the restaurant was open, its menu made full use of jail puns in names for the cuisine, and no, they didn't serve light bulbs. Tables sat inside the cells. *Texas Escapes* bestowed a Preservation Award to owners Steve Bell and Alan Walker "for their thorough and total reclamation."

---

After the restaurant closed, the building housed McAndrew's Bookshop & Cafe, but that closed, too. It's again on the market, and Ray Eckenrode, CCIM, of Appian Realty says, "In a city, recognized as fastest growing in the U.S., this three-story, totally refurbished 'Prison' is perfect for a restaurant." The building is listed on the web at: www.appiancommercial.com

*Crockett County Jail current appearance. Capt. Ron Hawthorne photographer.*

# Ozona
# Crockett County Jail
## (1892)
### near courthouse square

Modern Ozonans still point out the live oak tree where their founding fathers met in 1891 and mulled over the problem of what to do with lawbreakers. All they could do right then was to order a set of handcuffs and a couple of pairs of leg irons. But the very next year they built such a good jail it's still in use. Current Sheriff Shane Fenton says the tall tower never served its purpose as a gallows, and the jail was only filled to capacity one time, after bank robbers were captured in 1954. Around 1915 kids learned to play the piano in jail—where the sheriff's wife taught music lessons. Former Sheriff Billy Mills' kids immortalized their names in the concrete of the sidewalk.

A trustee's favorite story involved a prisoner, locked up for stealing a lawn mower. They finally had to release the suspect for want of evidence, since the lawn mower (a goat, it was learned later) had been cooked and eaten.

*Fort Bend County Jail current appearance. Photograph by Barclay Gibson.*

# Richmond
# Fort Bend County Jail
# (1896)

## the six-block Richmond Historic District near Houston

The arrangement of the Fort Bend County Jail is typical of jails built in the late 19th century. The sheriff's quarters are on the first floor, with jail cells on the second. Even the third floor hanging tower was to be expected. But since the two hangings conducted at this location, things have not been the same. Local historian and author John Allwright recounts that the last words of one convicted man were to admit his crime. The last words of the second man were to proclaim his innocence. Every month after that, on the date of the hanging, prisoners reported the sounds of groaning and a snap, like the sound of a neck breaking. The sheriff's family moved out in 1914, and no other family moved in, though no documentation tells why.

Caught up in Houston's urban sprawl, Richmond's historic buildings could have been razed to make way for "progress" had it not been for the creation of the Richmond Historic District. To do this, the Fort Bend Museum Association (www.fortbendmuseum.org/historicrichmond) and the City of Richmond made agreements on the adaptive re-use of certain buildings to save them. One such adaptation was for the Old Fort Bend County Jail to become the Richmond Police Department in 1999. Through cooperation of the city and museum, Richmond Historic District Commission reviews construction plans and building improvements within its district. And the handsome old jail still stands—eerie sounds and all.

# Waxahachie
# Ellis County Jail
## (1881)
### near courthouse

Of the almost extinct rotary cell jails built in America, Waxahachie has one of the few left. But, alas, the internal construction that made it rare is only a memory (for more on this technology, see the Denison: Grayson County chapter). It closed down after a new jail was built in 1929, but at least the building remains, still a beautiful credit to the town. In 1941, when the World War II scrap metal drive began, the commissioners accepted a contractor's bid for $7.10 per ton to remove the fifty tons of steel from the old jail. Since then, the building has been used for various businesses, most recently, Citizens National Bank.

In cooperation with that owner, Historic Waxahachie, Inc., hopes to find tenants to open such enterprises as art galleries, antiques, and other shops. The main goal of this organization is to see the building preserved and restored to as near its original appearance as possible. At present the building is structurally sound and is part of the Ellis County Courthouse Historical District.

# JAIL PRETENDING

*Hooters™ in Selma, Texas. Photograph by Louree and Charles Upton.*

## Selma
# Hooters™ Bar & Grill
### 15412 I-35 North

Mention old jails, and people often ask, "How about Hooters in Selma?" Its high-profile location fronts I-35 barely north of San Antonio, and its window bars and neon signs grab you by the optic nerve. Practically everybody around there "remembers" when it used to be a jail. Or did it?

In reality it started out as the WOAI radio station and later became the City Hall. But Captain Albert Zuniga of the Selma Police Department, who regularly brought prisoners in for booking, says the only way they could hold them was to handcuff them to the furniture. There were no cells. This was a tri-county facility for Bexar, Guadalupe, and Comal Counties. The cell now in place wasn't installed until a private owner bought the building and turned it into the City Bar & Grill, and then placed a table inside the cell. You have to hand it to that proprietor and Hooters for their sense of fun. Where else can you have a delicious meal inside a jail cell?

# JAIL RESIDENCE
## At least the building,

*Famed photographer Wyman Meinzer turned the Benjamin Jail into his home sweet home, which has been featured on HGTV.*

# JAILS ABANDONED

*Kent County Jail current appearance. Steve Neubauer photographer.*

*Moore County Jail current appearance. Judy and John Milam photographers.*

*New Boston City Jail current appearance. Joan May photographer.*

# GLOSSARY

*Corrugated ceiling at Henrietta a "greeter" hangs out to welcome guests.*
*Stacey Hasbrook photographer.*

**Corrugated steel ceilings** are almost a given in jails. Wherever you see these steel arches, you know they support concrete floors above that prevented prisoners from digging their way out.

**Graffiti** goes with the territory in jails where prisoners had time on their hands and emotions to vent. Some restorations have "repaired" and painted over "the damage." But as one curator said, "That too is history." He solved the problem of language and pictures that would be offensive to children and the general public by covering such sections with informative and entertaining posters.

**Hoosegow and calaboose** are two of the many slang words for jail. These came from butchered Spanish during the days of the Old West. Hoosegow for *juzgado* meant "a tribunal," (the local courthouse), but frontier justice warped the term into a synonym for jail. Likewise *calabozo*, usually a dungeon, became calaboose.

**Ironed** meant having leg irons, and sometimes wrist irons, welded on with chains attached to lessen chances of escape.

**Lever systems** outside a cell block would open or close all cell doors at once. The unique clanking sound of this device gave rise to the term of a jail as a "slammer," in effect signaling the finality between freedom and incarceration.

**Rising damp** has undermined several old structures. Without a barrier to ground moisture, masonry can't "breathe," and thus many a brick or adobe wall has crumbled from ground level up. Restoration efforts have often learned about the problems of rising damp the hard way.

**Riveted strap-iron cell** construction came before welding was possible. Cells were built of thick metal strips, riveted together in a painstaking way. The metal was heated red hot, borax

*A riveted strap-iron cell with a squint in the door at Granbury.*

poured into it, and the rivet hammered in to fuse the parts together. This kind of cell is easy to spot, and any welding you see was done at a later time.

**Rotary cell** or **squirrel-cage jails** were one of the most elaborate experiments in jail design. The Pauly Jail Manufacturing Company reports only about eighteen ever built in the U.S. (two in Texas). The Denison chapter explains more about this type of jail design.

**Runaround or runabout** meant an exercise area for nonviolent prisoners, sometimes a large open area or the walkway around cell cages, which had to be wide enough so prisoners couldn't grab jailers or other prisoners walking past.

**Saw-proof bars** were round with floating rods inside that would rotate with a saw stroke instead of being cut, as the older style solid bars could be.

**Sheriff** is a term that originated in Great Britain when King Alfred the Great (849-899) organized areas, much like our counties, into *shires*, which were headed by a *reeve*. The *shire reeve* was the chief law-enforcer, among other duties. Colonists to America brought with them the concept and term, which came to be pronounced *sheriff*.

**Squint** is the barred enclosure at eye level that sticks out in a cellblock door to allow a jailer to safely put his head into it and look to right and left, ensuring no prisoner will be hiding against the wall to ambush him.

**Stock** are steel bars manufactured with oil in a particular way to make the bars saw proof.